About Island Press

Since 1984, the nonprofit organization Island Press has been stimulating, shaping, and communicating ideas that are essential for solving environmental problems worldwide. With more than 1,000 titles in print and some 30 new releases each year, we are the nation's leading publisher on environmental issues. We identify innovative thinkers and emerging trends in the environmental field. We work with world-renowned experts and authors to develop cross-disciplinary solutions to environmental challenges.

Island Press designs and executes educational campaigns in conjunction with our authors to communicate their critical messages in print, in person, and online using the latest technologies, innovative programs, and the media. Our goal is to reach targeted audiences—scientists, policymakers, environmental advocates, urban planners, the media, and concerned citizens—with information that can be used to create the framework for long-term ecological health and human well-being.

Island Press gratefully acknowledges major support of our work by The Agua Fund, The Andrew W. Mellon Foundation, The Bobolink Foundation, The Curtis and Edith Munson Foundation, Forrest C. and Frances H. Lattner Foundation, The JPB Foundation, The Kresge Foundation, The Oram Foundation, Inc., The Overbrook Foundation, The S.D. Bechtel, Jr. Foundation, The Summit Charitable Foundation, Inc., and many other generous supporters.

The opinions expressed in this book are those of the author(s) and do not necessarily reflect the views of our supporters.

WILD
BY DESIGN

WILD
BY DESIGN

STRATEGIES FOR CREATING LIFE-ENHANCING LANDSCAPES

MARGIE RUDDICK

ISLANDPRESS Washington | Covelo | London

Island Press is a trademark of The Center for Resource Economics.

Library of Congress Control Number: 2015950738

 Printed on recycled, acid-free paper

Manufactured in the United States of America
10 9 8 7 6 5 4 3 2 1

Keywords: Baja, beauty, biodiversity, Chengdu, China, climate change, coastal protection, Coney Island, conservation, ecology, expression, flooding, Governors Island, green infrastructure, habitat, health, India, Kinderhook, landscape architecture, levee, Liberty State Park, living machine, Living Water Park, mental health, Miami Beach, natural infrastructure, New York City, park, particulate matter, Philadelphia, Queens Plaza, recreation, regeneration, reinvention, resilience, restoration, shade, Shillim Retreat and Institute, Staten Island, stewardship, stormwater, sustainable design, Urban Garden Room, urbanization, water quality, Western Ghats

To parents,
stewards,
teachers,
students,
children—

all children,
and mine.

CONTENTS

Preface

For a half century, a stretch of Route 1 that runs through Saugus, Massachusetts, just north of Boston, was lit up by the giant glass saguaro cactus in front of Hilltop Steakhouse. The aging highway strip also included the Kowloon Polynesian Restaurant (with an immense tiki god smiling out at the parking lot), and a mini-golf sporting brightly colored dinosaurs. The inventive signs that had sprouted up on the strip over the years seemed to appeal to even the most discerning urbanite; people came from all over to dine on Route 1. But the actual landscape could not have been bleaker: crumbling roadway, acres of empty parking lots, newer big-box retail with all the not-so-hidden loading docks. It may not have been the kind of landscape that would be considered a good fit as the subject of a design studio in landscape architecture at Harvard's Graduate School of Design 10 years ago, when I was a visiting critic. But that is exactly what I proposed.

In all fairness, its didactic potential took me decades to discover. I had been familiar with this commercial strip since I was in college; every time I did the late-night run from my college in Maine back home to New York, or to Boston for a big-city weekend, I loved peering out the Greyhound bus window at this sparkling Vegas of the Northeast. In graduate school as well, the strip played a prominent role in my life: After staying up all night several days in a row for a design review, a particularly brutal hazing ritual that persists to this day, my friends and I would pile into a couple of cars and make the drive from Boston out to Hilltop, to savor 22-ounce steaks served with nuclear-scaled baked potatoes and individual side salads made up of half-heads of iceberg topped with Italian dressing.

I loved this particular strip. It was totally out of character for button-down Boston. It was all light and color and people knocking each other over stampeding for tables. But only a short time before the Harvard Graduate School of Design (GSD) studio, after countless encounters with this land-

Hilltop Steakhouse,
Saugus, Massachusetts.

scape, I noticed something else. One wintry day, as I was driving at a snail's pace in order not to skid off the road, a toddler in the child's seat behind me, I looked for the first time through the icy parking lots sprouted with these sculptural buildings and signs.

And I noticed something I had never seen before: Behind and slightly downhill from this world of highway and boxes for consuming were wetlands and what looked like a river snaking its way toward the ocean.

I would never before have guessed that if, when we got out of our cars at Kowloon Polynesian Restaurant, we had turned left rather than right, we would have ended up in one of the largest wetland reserves in the Northeast. When I got home I looked for some maps of the area (this was before GoogleEarth) and discovered that it included four major park reserves, several cemeteries, a quarry, and the Saugus River, which runs under Route 1 right in the middle of this amazing strip to meet the ocean less than a mile away.

How extraordinary to have a network of wild reserves surrounding this wild strip of human artifice. This is what made the landscape seem worth studying. Before, it had interested me because it's a place I love, in addition to the fact that struggling smaller-scale highway retail is a landscape type in desperate need of reinvention. But the confluence with an immense natural water ecosystem gave another dimension to the landscape and a new aspect worth studying.

Not everyone saw its potential. When the chair of the landscape architecture department at the GSD called me up the next month to ask whether I had a studio I could teach, I immediately thought of Route 1 and my recent discovery. There was silence on the other end of the phone. At that time, visiting critics usually flew in from out of town to lead really sexy studios that took students to Barcelona, for instance, or Beijing. After clearing his throat, the chair explained to me that most students were interested in serious design studios or, he implied, at least projects that didn't land them on a bleak strip of asphalt less than 10 miles from the school. I didn't hear back.

But a couple of years later, in 2007, a new chair was transforming the GSD's landscape architecture department into a paragon of sustainable design. Urban wetlands and community gardens were in. Blank-slate design was out. Ecological design was, at least in principle, back.

So when the new chair called me up to ask whether I was interested in teaching a studio, I again suggested Route 1 where the Hilltop Steakhouse lights up the night. This time, I got a positive response.

The GSD chair's support was one thing, but I still needed students. I had to present at the open lottery for all studios, along with an offering in architecture that was going to investigate "the conditionality of the ceiling." Despite my worry that I would attract no students to my little strip project, a handful seemed to get what fascinated me about the place. They threw themselves into the place and the work with abandon. I was thrilled.

The students immersed themselves in the ecology, economics, and cultural background of the area. Their projects looked at how to transform this strip, from rethinking the program, creating more housing and offices, to building wildlife bridges. Two themes ran through every student's scheme: the matrix of wetland and woodland that the students discovered on foot, and fell in love with, and the aesthetic of the strip, or rather developing an aesthetic that would integrate commerce, driving, and nature. These particular students could balance these two themes, the ecological and the design agendas, or rather tolerate and even cultivate a tension between the two. Their schemes were beautiful, arresting.

The ideas we discussed and wrestled with in that Route 1 studio were the initial inspirations for this book. As I worked on it over the years, I thought about how to give it a title that would describe what we were doing, engaging in both the science of the environment and also the art part. I couldn't come up with anything except this question: "What Are We Doing Here, Anyway?"

The book was something of a response to all the checklists that had proliferated in the new millennium. The Leadership in Energy and Environmental Design (LEED), a guideline for sustainable practices begun in 1998 but really formalized in 2005, had codified "green practices," with checklists that designers followed, gaining points for sustainable practices and winning a platinum or gold or silver LEED certification. Developers had started to market their LEED rating as a sales angle. My experience was that LEED was designed so that designers would do no harm or do less harm. However, the guidelines were so global—"don't build within x number of feet of a wetland," for example—that innovative design that would integrate a new wetland with the built world, bridging the nature–culture divide, was enjoined from some creative and novel solutions. So I started to ask myself, "What are we doing here? Are we saving the planet or are we making something?" The implicit answer was that we were making art and we were engaging in ecological design.

For the next couple of years, I spent time looking at all the projects I had done over the years and tried to come up some sort of system for the process. I started to enumerate the things we were doing, in a prescriptive way, like LEED, but not intended as hard-and-fast rules. The ensuing titles, such as "Cleaning Up Messes," that recur throughout the text are intended only as suggestion, not command. The title for the book remained "What Are We Doing Here, Anyway?"—a little unwieldy, but it kept me asking the questions that kept challenging any formula for "green."

I'd been working intermittently on the manuscript for a few years when, in 2011, I had another perspective-shifting experience in another landscape I was familiar with: my yard. I had been conducting an ad hoc reforestation project over the past 6 years when I received a summons for allowing weeds in my front yard to grow higher than the 10 inches allowed by the Department of Licenses and Inspection for the City of Philadelphia.

The story became viral among my colleagues, and Anne Raver wrote a piece for the *New York Times* on my home landscape—part reforestation project, part domestic garden—with the title "In Philadelphia a Garden Grows Wild." I received e-mails from around the world, some saying things like "Thank God someone understands my approach to gardening." I discovered that I had tapped into a huge movement, the wild gardening movement. I started to understand that what I and my students, and many of my peers, had been doing here was making landscapes that were both wild and clearly designed. Not faux nature but also not slavishly ordered. A little messy but not too much. Intentionally and carefully designed. And, in the best of circumstances, lovingly maintained.

I don't know when the title "Wild by Design" popped into my head, but once it did everyone got it immediately. "That's what I have been trying to do," many of them told me.

I hope this book will give readers an idea of how they might try to bridge the two realms that were traditionally held distant: the hyper-orderly and aestheticized world of designers, and the sometimes mucky but exquisitely beautiful world of ecologists. This book is an encouragement for people to devise their own paths in making change to the environment, not only to follow their preferred or mandated checklists, like LEED, but also to draw from a flexible framework that begins with following their own intuition and their own way of reading the landscape; to tap into the myriad seemingly imperceptible webs and networks that make a place what it is; to follow their passion for landscape, which drove them to their chosen fields or avocations and which, I hope, spurred them to look at this book and think it might be relevant to their work and their lives.

Casa Finisterra,
Baja California.

How Did We Get Here?

Landscape architecture. Is it art? Is it ecology? This has been the struggle for almost 50 years. Every landscape architect or designer today finds herself at some point reckoning with where she sits on the spectrum between the two. It used to be easier: There were the design mavens, such as Peter Walker, formalists who concerned themselves largely with the way a landscape looked, whether it was striped or curvy. Then there were the ecologists, such as the practice Andropogon, who, although they do pursue a formal agenda, give the way a landscape works ecologically primacy over empty form.

But in the age of sustainability, ecological principles have been institutionalized, metabolized into the practice so that few people dare to design a landscape that does not in some way respond to natural forces such as sun or wind. The field is much murkier, with formally oriented designers by necessity deploying ecological principles and ecologically oriented designers drawing on recent precedents of formally strong *and* ecologically sound projects. But the wild part in fact can be a product of design, and the design part can be wild.

Often when I teach first-year landscape architecture students, I start by asking them to make a conceptual model of the landscape that formed them, from childhood or later. They almost invariably respond with natural, or seemingly natural, landscapes: the creek behind their house, or the beach they went to, or the park that they thought was natural-made, and within that park, a woodland where they played. Sometimes they refer to an obviously constructed landscape, such as a farm. But they rarely refer to a garden, or a plaza, or a formally ordered park. More often than not, the primal landscape that planted the seed of environmental design in us is one that is wild.

Naturally occurring grove, Kinderhook, New York.

But when I ask students what they studied in high school or college that led them to the field, or just what they loved to do, I find some who come from a science background, but more often than not, students have had some art practice, whether it is painting, sculpture, or ceramics. Equally powerful in channeling someone into the field of landscape architecture is a drive to make things, to order the world formally according to rules and habits we devise as humans. The curriculum of landscape architecture schools is heavily weighted toward the making of things. Most programs determine that the studio course, where design happens, should take up 75 percent of the student's time; the other 25 percent is to be spent on at least three core or elective courses. We communicate—and we create—through drawings and models, far more than through words.

This duality—a love of the "natural" landscape and a love of making things—is paralleled by a long-held belief that there is a duality between what is "natural" and what is constructed.

"Natural": forest, Western Ghats of India.

"Constructed": median, Queens Plaza.

For generations, landscape architects have been trying to bridge these two realms—the "built" realm and the seemingly natural one—in design, so people do not think that this streetscape in New York City and this woodland floor in the Western Ghats of India have nothing to do with each other. In fact they are related, not just because they both react to changes in the actions of the sun or the amount of rain that falls. The "naturalness" of this forest floor does not immediately let on that people have dwelled and sustained themselves in this forest for eons. It would not exist as it does without humans, and humans would not exist without the forest, where they gather plants for food, medicine, and fuel. And as for the streetscape, the plants were selected to handle the increased heat of urban pavements, salts in winter; to survive the impact of people walking, running, riding their bikes, driving their cars. The plantings provide habitat for birds and butterflies, among other animals and insects. They filter dirty stormwater. If that is not operating as a "natural" system, I don't know what is.

In the past decade or so, the term *sustainability*—illustrated by this diagram that shows how economics and culture (or "society") should be constrained by environmental concerns—has become the umbrella under which this knitting back together of the ideas of the built world and the natural world has flourished. But what we are doing is not new. In the field of landscape planning and design, in the decade since sustainability gained currency we have just brought to the foreground what designers were doing for ages. You can look back to the great landscapes of the Loire in France, those vast water gardens, and see an expression of the hydrology of the valley. Only recently did we break the connection between where we live and how nature operates. In the past decade we have seen a shift from formally oriented landscapes that waste resources such as energy and water to landscapes that showcase native plants, survive with low maintenance, and rely on gravity rather than electric pumps to move water, for instance. Natural processes are in; wasteful decadence is out.

Sustainability Venn diagram.

The chateaux of the Loire Valley, such as Chenonceau, express the power of the river.

But looking at this image of a chateau in the Loire Valley, you can see a merging of the impulse to make something fantastical with the energies of the site, the water that courses through it. *The next generation in design will be reinventing this connection between the ecology of a site and the expression of a culture.* Fifteen years ago, designers rarely worked on projects that pushed the natural processes of the site to the foreground. It is now up to the coming generations of designers to retrieve the other drivers that have always worked on us from the background: culture, society, and art. Since the rise of ecology and the advent of Leadership in Energy and Environmental Design (LEED), which puts designers through their sustainable practices paces and only marginally addresses form or aesthetics, form has taken a backseat to sustainability. Quite often, the way a project works is assigned a higher value than the way it looks and feels. Anyone who went into the design field as a visual, formal practice might wonder whether that should be the case.

Landscape as a Living Machine

So how did we get here, to a place where ecology can have primacy over the art of what we do?

At many American colleges, over the past decade the number of students enrolled in environmental science classes has doubled, and it has tripled at some. The message of Earth Day 1970 has finally hit the mainstream, and the average American values the idea of sustainability. Recycling is part of the culture now; bike sharing and making do without cars are movements that are gaining ground.

Living machine at the Living Water Park, Chengdu, Sichuan, China.

So now it's feasible, not only technologically but culturally, to make a park that filters polluted river water naturally, through wetlands. Such practices now represent the mainstream in our field. The Living Water Park, in Chengdu, Sichuan, China, which environmental artist Betsy Damon invited me to help design in 1996, demonstrates how water can be cleansed biologically, filtered through a series of settlement ponds, constructed wetlands, and aeration surfaces.

In 1996 a lot of my colleagues thought I was a little crazy to go work on a project in China about cleaning water, particularly a project for which I would get paid very little.

But in the past several years US health and stormwater codes have changed to reflect a growing understanding of the positive impact of low-tech green practices on the building, the landscape, and the larger ecological systems surrounding us. Ten years ago, in most US counties, if you wanted to treat a building's wastewater biologically, through reed beds and aeration systems, you had to build a second, conventional system as a backup, in case the sustainable system failed. It was very hard to convince clients to spend up to twice the cost of a conventional system, for a system of which many government agency officials were extremely wary.

But by 2011, the idea of a living machine, a system that cleanses water through settlement, aeration, and filtration, was not so far out: There were at least twenty-five living machines in the United States as of 2014, filtering all the wastewater—gray water from sinks and showers, black water from toilets—through constructed wetlands, cleansing and polishing it until it is clean enough to drink.

The living machines that are up and running in the United States—not only at progressive institutions such as Oberlin and Berea Colleges but also in the City of South Burlington, Vermont—really work. Now that sustainable design is mainstream, some of us are more comfortable with the idea of our waste being recycled through our own front yards, and designs such as the improvements to Queens Plaza in New York City are common. Permeable paving reduces the load of stormwater that flows into our streams, lakes, and oceans; rain gardens retain stormwater and allow the groundwater to recharge.

The resulting landscape looks different from a more conventional streetscape. It is greener, not only because the retained stormwater cultivates lusher plantings and permeable pavers reduce the amount of water sheeting across our pavements but because choices of materials—from light-colored pavers that reduce the heat island effect by reflecting sunlight to recycled concrete salvaged from old streets and sidewalks—reduce our ecological footprint.

The practices that have come to be called sustainable reduce the need for large water infrastructure, such as underground pipes and ducts that not only are vulnerable to earthquakes and other events but also speed the movement of water to our creeks, streams, rivers, and oceans. These practices reduce our need for manufacturing and transporting materials. They create healthier places for wildlife as well as people. These practices are intended to protect and heal the earth, which includes us.

The advent of sustainable landscape design happened to coincide with the arrival of a kind of minimalist modernism as the formal idiom of the day. In the first decade of the sustainable landscape movement, many designers, if not most, took their formal cues from minimalism: broad swaths of reed beds, smooth concrete edges. The processes—water flow and plant growth, for example—were foregrounded. The will to make something, to engage in the practice of design as an artistic expression, was pushed into the background. Looking at professional magazines from 2007 on reveals a preoccupation with the clean lines of modernism and the process of water cleansing.

The practical measures of sustainable design make the landscape function more efficiently and reduce the amount of wasted materials and energy; they are conceived to contribute to the overall health of the planet rather than detract. But without an artistic or cultural component to the landscape, we are creating natural places that function like machines. A truly sustainable place works on a more visceral level. We are transforming places so people will love them, will take better care of them, will want them to flourish for their grandchildren and their grandchildren's grandchildren. If we just look at what are called "best practices," meaning the technologies that are accepted as most environmentally healthful, we still would not necessarily know how to make a landscape that people will internalize, make their own. Sustainability is about people taking ownership, learning how to sustain, rather than abuse or just consume, the landscape. It is about making clear the connection between human practices and our environment.

The field of landscape architecture can make these connections between humans and our environment. Over generations the discipline has careened from one set of formal goals to another. The nineteenth century popularized the romantic conception of landscape as a wild place to encounter the sublime, which had its apotheosis in Olmsted. The formalist Beaux Arts movement in landscape architecture drew on the rational geometries of Renaissance and Baroque design to create a perfectly ordered world (think of the 1893 Chicago World's Fair); the modern landscape movement took the landscape as a canvas or three-dimensional material with which to make a work of art. The conception of the landscape as a living organism only gained currency in the 1960s and could be said to have gone underground again in the 1980s.

Contemporary photograph of the Ravine, Central Park.

In the United States, the field of landscape architecture has traditionally played a key role in the making of our environments. From Central Park to the lazy meanders of subdivisions to the poetic curves of the Blue Ridge Parkway, landscape architects did the studies, laid the ideas down on paper, and oversaw construction. For over a century, the conception of the landscape in parks and natural areas focused on the quiet and serene enjoyment of scenery. Parks such as Central Park, which many people today would consider a "natural" park, were in fact artificially constructed to give people a heightened sense of rock and water and greenery, counteracting the damaging effects, to the psyche and to the body, of the conditions in overcrowded and dirty industrializing cities.

NORTHERN WHITE CEDAR
DOMINANT

NORTHERN WHITE
CEDAR DOMINANT

DECIDUOUS
DOMINANT

G R A Z I N G   A R E A

Bio-map, northwestern
Connecticut.

But by the 1960s, the "style" of the picturesque landscape had become static, a rigid, if curvy, style that often did not relate to the conditions of the site itself. Ian McHarg, the author of *Design with Nature*, promoted a new way of intervening in the landscape, building up layers of scientific data to determine where the best place is to build, which areas to avoid, how to protect watersheds and fragile microclimates. A generation of architects and planners was converted to the McHargian overlay system, in which "objective" decisions about where to build and how and what to build (responding to nature) were made thanks to a huge, unwieldy computer program or many hours of creating acetate overlays in design offices. The romance that had faded from the picturesque landscape, which by the 1960s had become a formula, was reignited in McHarg's love affair with nature.

In a predictable swing of the pendulum, the design generation after McHarg, at least those attracted to architecture and landscape architecture as a formal discipline, began to revolt. By the 1990s the ecological approach had come to be identified as "nondesign," a kind of crunchy granola, nature-designing-itself, politically correct dogma. Heavy-hitting designers such as Peter Walker rebelled against the ecological doctrine, focusing on landscape as art. Environmental artists such as Mary Miss, Nancy Holt, Alan Sonfist, and Robert Smithson seemed to be able to get at the nature of place through a poetic or minimal language.

When I was in graduate school in the late 1980s, the pinnacle of practice seemed to be the blank-slate site. When you hang out your shingle, the trajectories of our high-design elders implied, you do increasingly expensive private projects until you get famous. Then you get yourself hired by a developer or a municipality; you are given a rectangle, or a complex of shapes in plan, to make a landscape; you do your thing. The stripes of Peter Walker, the tire palm grids of Martha Schwartz reflect more a process of invention than reinvention. These projects occurred mostly on green-field sites, and although many practitioners such as Martha Schwartz actually spent a good deal of time on site analysis—understanding topography and plantings, for example—you may not know it looking at the delightful geometries and juxtapositions that resulted. The preexisting site rarely read through the graphic solution, because the preexisting site was often a flat, undifferentiated plane ripe for development.

Peter Walker,
Sony Centers,
Berlin.

My only encounter with Norman Newton, author of *Design on the Land* and himself a product of Beaux Arts training, occurred in graduate school, when one of our younger teachers assigned us a triangular site, a leftover wedge surrounded by roadways, home to a Gulf service station, to reinvent as housing with gardens. Watching the students agonizing, contorting themselves trying to justify the odd geometries—shoehorning circles and boxes and axes and spirals and all manner of forms into one mean little triangle—he shuffled from desk to desk mercilessly slamming every single student's work. Finally one brazen student asked him why he was trashing everyone. His answer: "This site has terrible geometry." "So what would you do if you were hired for this project?" she followed up with. "It's a bad site! I would reject the commission!" he thundered.

Getting Beyond the Idea of Good and Bad

But by the late 1980s, the idea of good sites and bad sites on which to practice your artful manipulation of form had passed out of favor, or just out of reality. By the late 1980s, young practitioners were as likely to be handed a "good geometry," green-field site to design as they were a garden to design for the King of Morocco. In the early 1990s our first public projects—the projects for which young designers competed fiercely—often dealt with the marginal spaces left over once the infrastructure of the 1950s and 1960s, lines of roadway slicing through our cities, had started to degrade. Many of our projects reclaimed brownfield sites just coming available through the Superfund and other remediation programs. Elevated roadway and railway sites, vacant lots, and toxic landfills became our stock-in-trade. The landscape solutions to the problem of how to make these spaces more livable, or return them to public use, involved a process of reinvention: You can't make that highway overpass go away, so how does your design solution reposition it, recast it as something beautiful or healthful?

When well-known Japanese landscape architect Toru Mitani was in graduate school, he took a seminar on environmental art. For his final presentation, when all his classmates had assembled trays and trays of slides showing desert cuts and spiraling jetties for their talks, he presented only one slide: a power line.

A power line: beautiful or toxic?

Mitani's entire presentation consisted of the following three sentences: "When I was a little boy, I thought this was the most beautiful thing in the world, this structure. . . . Then in the 1970s I learned that in fact it was not beautiful, that it was toxic and gave people cancer. . . . Now I have come to graduate school and I am learning that this structure is beautiful."

An entire thesis in three sentences.

The emerging minimalism of the 1990s—represented by landscape architects' and architects' interest in the serial work of Donald Judd and Carl Andre and in the installations of Michael Heizer and Mary Miss, among others— embraced infrastructure as something beautiful. The architecture of the power line was not something to hide, to doll up to look like something else, or to relegate to the margins, as much planning of the 1950s and 1960s did. Infrastructure was something that, if reinvented in a new context of an artful landscape, had an impressive toughness, a rigor to its rhythms. This is not to imply that the process of reinvention was anything new; Central Park is only the most famous pastoral park to have resulted from a reinvention of its preexisting topography and water courses. But as the need to recast our urban edges and infrastructures became the primary generator of leading-edge public projects, the "blank slate" approach to landscape began to wither and die.

Focusing on What's There

The idea of site-specific design gained currency as sites that came up for funding grew ever more complex. There was no formula for how a project on a marginal site should be designed. Not that landscape traditions of the past can be called formulaic. But by the 1980s many of these traditions—pastoral, Beaux Arts, modern—had been mindlessly replicated for so many generations that they had come to seem banal. Yet looking at how some of the most seemingly banal landscape forms were born, you can see how when a widely publicized, often brilliant and inspired design solution is mindlessly replicated, it turns into a formula with no context. The City Beautiful movement often drew on existing axes and vistas to arrive at pure formal beauty in the plan layout of boulevards and avenues. Imitators replicated plans in new places, creating geometries based on nothing other than a drawing seen in a book or library. The first kidney-shaped swimming pool grew out of Tommy Church's desire to pull the curving wetland visible off in the distance into the foreground of a coastal site in California. When you see the pool with the wetland in the background and the organic sculpture hovering at the water line you can see how Church reinvented the site as part of a much larger landscape; how he restored the connection between the site and the water; how he expressed something fundamental about the flow of organic forms on this wetland edge, at the same time that he was expressing the formal spirit of modernism in the clean, bold, almost graphic lines.

It was only when people started to copy his pool, slapping kidney-shaped pools into every suburban lot regardless of context or scale, that this form became formula, losing its grounding in site and spirit. There is nothing inventive about a kidney-shaped pool now. But the original not only reinvented its coastal site, it reinvented the practice of landscape design for many years to come.

For many, LEED reinvented the practice of landscape architecture, and architecture, to forge a new connection between built form and the environment. It has now become the norm. How do we integrate these traditions into our own work, so that we are not simply following the latest how-to manual—the LEED checklist, for instance—but getting to the deeper sense of the landscape and of stewardship, in which connection, form, and craftsmanship are in some quarters valued as highly as the number of sustainability points achieved? In the pages that follow, I call out the operations I think we are following, from collaborating with others to restoring meadows. I use the gerund form to call out what we are doing, avoiding the imperative that would prescribe what the reader should do. That way, the question that became the working title of this book—What are we doing here, anyway?—is kept alive throughout the book and I hope in the reader's mind, while allowing the reader to come up with his or her own answers to the question.

But that is only one of the questions we ask ourselves when undertaking any project. When we start any project the first question we ask is, "Where am I?" What is the nature of this place? What is it about the way the landscape is designed, built, or used that makes a place recognizable, unique, cherished? It is important that we understand our own biases and shortcomings, too, in order to devise a process that can be truly present for the place, the client, the program. To do this it is most instructive to start by trying to understand our own landscape, the place where we live. Most designers come face to face with who we are, what we really believe in, and what we are capable of when we have the chance to design our own environments. If you want to understand what someone really values and believes as a designer, it sometimes helps to look at the place where they live. The evolution of the small yard around my ranch house outside Philadelphia has played an outsized role in helping me develop my own strategies and process, as I explain in the next chapter.

The original kidney-shaped pool was designed in response to the form of coastal wetlands in the background.

The author's home
landscape, year 4.

Chapter 1:

A Laboratory for Wild By Design

The lessons of my own landscape helped me develop a set of rules for how to let a wild landscape emerge: Let things happen, but make sure it looks intentional, so as not just to let things go; try not to create mess in other people's yards; get help. But there is also the design part, which is where the strategies in the chapters to follow come in. You can't just plant a lot of stuff and let it go. The wild garden, or the eco-park, or the eco-city, needs a lot of tending, coddling, nurturing, and sometimes brutal hacking back, in order for it not to devolve completely into a massive tangle of trees, shrubs, and vines.

In order to have a "wild garden" and not a seemingly abandoned lot, you need to walk the thin line between order and chaos. And you need to exercise a greater design hold than many would imagine. The landscapes I make have a strong formal structure, for the most part; at least that is another rule I follow that I sometimes break. A strong formal hand helps to bring out the wild: It is that structural order against which the wild is clearly visible.

The seeming "naturalness" is the product of watching, weeding, moving, adjusting.

I went to Harvard's Graduate School of Design, a school that at the time prioritized "design" over "ecology," from the Natural Resources Group in New York City, where I helped map the wetlands, woodlands, and meadows of the city's natural parklands. I don't attribute my career in landscape design to childhood visits to gardens; rather, I am certain that the wild beaches and back dunes of eastern Long Island, where I spent summers, planted in me the seeds of my vocation.

I have always loved wild places, urban or otherwise: the dunes and scrub of eastern Long Island, which I consider my native landscape; the Shoshone River in Wyoming's Tetons, where I spent two childhood summers; the Ramble in Central Park, where I worked in the mid-1980s. But until recently I didn't realize how much my work tries to capture, even for a brief moment, and even in the city, the feeling of being immersed in a raw, sometimes wild piece of nature. I didn't recognize how dualistic my own design process is, toeing the line between wildness and order. It was not until 2011, when my own domestic landscape was branded a "wild garden," that I started to connect the dots.

In the winter of 2005 I bought a ranch house in a leafy Philadelphia neighborhood. After living in Philadelphia twins, or duplexes, for a dozen years, it occurred to me that what I really needed was a ranch house: compact, efficient, manageable, with a free plan, like the New York apartment I grew up in. I wanted the inside/outside connection that made the ranch the ultimate California type.

As I surfed the Internet for ranch houses in my neighborhood, the perfect house popped up onto my computer screen: butt-ugly, beige and gray brick, sitting in the snow all by itself, but a compact three-bedroom with corner windows and space all around it and a lot of light and air inside. A visit revealed a warren of small rooms packed into the small footprint of less than 2,000 square feet, but the walls would be easy to pull down. My home renovation engine went into overdrive.

Home reforestation project: the awkward age.

However, my fine-tuned radar went blank when trained on what, given my career, some would assume to be the first thing I would tackle: the landscape. The little ranch sat on a third of an acre, with one large silver maple (twin leader, weak crotch) and two bedraggled native dogwoods in the side yard, struggling to survive the lower-limb blight that has taken so many of them down in these parts over the past decades. All else, save the house footprint, the double-wide driveway, and a couple of concrete paths and pads, was lawn. And not just any lawn but a carefully tended, tidied, and chemically enhanced lawn. Once spring arrived and I got a look at all those perfect emerald green blades pushing up from the thawing earth, I realized that we were in trouble: Major volumes of herbicides, fungicides, and othercides were probably deployed to make a lawn that green and unblemished. The spring thaw revealed a sign planted on one side of the lot advertising a national lawn care company with a chemical-sounding name.

People would come to visit, look at the blank rectangle of lawn, and say, "So, I bet you have big plans for the landscape, right?" Well, no, actually. It was a blank slate; I am a designer of the adaptive reuse era. Give me a blank slate and I will have no idea what to do. The same common phrase kept popping into my head: Don't do something, just stand there. So gradually, over the next 5 or 6 years, I inadvertently engineered my own private reforestation and garden project.

That first year I discovered, after one pass at mowing all that lawn, that there was no way I was going to spend over an hour a week mowing. I didn't even want all that lawn. So I figured out how much lawn I really needed— a front path, an ample side yard for games, enough lawn at the back so we could hang out—and made a mowing plan by walking the outline I wanted for the lawn with the mower. That one move, what could be called discerning mowing, stood in for a more strategic design process for the next 2 or 3 years.

Rethinking Lawn: Starting with Mowing Plans

Where I mowed the lawn, albeit unaerated, unfertilized, and otherwise untreated lawn, the short lawn remained, growing more mossy at shaded low points where it stayed dampest after rains and sprouting with dandelions, clover, and violets, as well as crabgrass and other "weeds," kept low by their weekly haircut. Where I didn't mow, the grasses and "weeds" grew knee high by July. Sometime around that time each summer I would catch someone, a friend or neighbor, or even a member of my own family, looking askance at my messy front yard, and I would quickly scout around for someone to come weed-whack the naturalizing lawn-turning-to-meadow. Often I would hijack a crew from a neighbor's yard, offering them $50, and they would go at it, but somehow, mysteriously, when I tried to get them back for another pass they would be tied up. My landscape scared even the landscapers.

In a bid to appease the neighbors and attract some skilled landscape help, I decided to clean up the edges of my messifying front yard. I mowed straight strips of meadow and overseeded them with turf grass, creating a tidy border around the property on the sidewalk and driveway sides, and a nice clean lawn path curving up from the sidewalk to the side yard. There, I told myself. Now it looks intentional.

Keeping the Edges Clean

In her book *Messy Ecosystems, Orderly Frames*, University of Michigan landscape architecture professor Joan Iverson Nassauer argues that although a messy groundplane promotes ecological health and even biodiversity, we

Roughly mown edges and a path up the middle of the space make the reforested patch (augmented with oakleaf hydrangea and ferns) appear more intentional.

are, at least as Americans, culturally averse to accepting the mess in our own back yards, or our neighbors'. She illustrates that a tidy margin of lawn, for instance, or the orderly frame of the title, increases people's comfort with a landscape that carries the "disorderliness" or mess that supports life. A landscape that has been let go or cultivated for habitat will receive more buy-in if the public edges are kept neat, framed by lawn, walkways, or other devices. I found that once I had mown clean edges my neighbors calmed down considerably. Letting things happen can be instructive and fruitful, but it also can look like you are just letting things go; put a tidy frame around it so it looks as planned and managed as it in fact will be.

By my third year of this experiment, the woody plants that had started to seed into the "meadow" began to harden off and show themselves. One whole bank of former lawn, where the side yard sloped down to the sidewalk, sprouted thick with black cherry seedlings, considered by many to be an invasive threat. Wild black cherry not only reproduce like mad, they also

In early spring the black cherry stand, left, is coppiced; the cherries, oaks, and other volunteers to the right are hand-pruned and underplanted with ferns, hellebores, and plants left over from the landscaper's other properties (a hosta can be seen poking out of the middle).

tend to be allelopathic: They send out into the earth at their base certain substances that discourage anything else from growing there. I knew that if I simply let them go, the bank would become a dark black cherry grove where little can grow on the groundplane, and the birds and the winds would broadcast black cherry seeds all over the neighborhood. My neighbors would not appreciate this, and I would just have this dark grove with little of the vertical layering that makes a landscape diverse. So I coppiced the whole stand, cut it down to about 3 feet high, and repeated whenever it looked like it might start to shoot out into a grove again, maybe several times a year.

Coppicing creates a bushy, thick habit, like a dense shrub layer. By cutting back in the spring, we prevent the trees from fruiting, lowering their value to birds, butterflies, and moths. But the practice achieves two important goals: The low, full stratum is home to many more species than a tall open woodland would be, and keeping the trees from producing berries keeps the plants from spreading throughout the neighborhood and beyond. In practice it is a rule, too often broken, that you do not change the topography of your property to send water to a neighbor's land; you do not empty a swimming pool (if you have one) by placing the vacuum hose end directed toward someone else's land. The same should go for dispersing invasive species, although in practice that takes a lot of maintenance. My property is a source of Norway maple, Japanese maple, and other invasive types, but I don't have the heart or the means to remove them completely.

Keeping Stuff We Don't Want off the Neighbors' Property

The regeneration in the front yard was more mixed, because it gets more sunlight—black cherries, but also grasses and sedges that started to turn my front yard into a real meadow. Or so it appeared to me; some people still thought our place looked abandoned, and occasionally strangers would walk right up to the windows and look in to see whether the house was for sale.

That third summer I decided to make a vegetable plot in the front, and I planted a couple rows of tomatoes, and zinnias, and pumpkins for the fall. Kids loved it. Although the emerging forest/coppice had yet to achieve the look of something anyone could name, in the meantime this part of what was the front lawn had become a field.

The street often isn't visible,
to the left, beyond the veg-
etable/flower/herb patch.

Exporting Less

The next summer I started to add native plants at some of the edges, to provide a little color and screening of the chain link stretch of back fence—Carolina allspice, oakleaf hydrangea, and a variety of viburnums—and to start to articulate the spaces that were emerging through my mowing patterns. I planted a mix of aronia and leatherleaf viburnum to screen the two back corners (one the leaf pile, the other the brush pile) and the short side of the house, to keep the tools, containers from plantings, and compost bins out of sight. I finally had enough land, and two back corners that could use rounding off, to turn to larger-scale composting than just kitchen waste. More to spread around the garden, less to send to the landfill. Regardless of how many branches felled by winter storms we piled onto the brush pile or loads of leaves dumped onto the leaf pile, by the end of the winter it always seemed as if the pile was the same height as the year before. Gone were branches stuffed into trash bins on trash day; gone were the lines of brown leaf bags. I had composted kitchen waste for years; if we could just stop buying packaged goods and receiving mail we would be able to stop all curbside pickups.

In the front garden the selection of greens, flowers, and herbs, as well as hardy ground covers, needs very little water or weeding.

Late that third summer I sensed that my neighbors, who were grumbling about this mess of a yard, would appreciate some splashes of color, more as an indication that someone was home than as a floral display, so I planted fall asters in small masses, along the short driveway and the sidewalk. I mowed a path up the middle of the front yard, separating the coppiced black cherries from the more mixed successional path nearer the driveway. I planted oakleaf hydrangeas along the paths. The place started to look lived in and layered. Instead of a big rectangle with a box on it, my landscape evolved into a series of places you might want to be in, whether to garden in the front, hang out in the back yard, or toss a football in the side yard.

Old oil vats were adapted for a water garden.

The next two summers I expanded the vegetable patch, and in the chaotic-seeming meadow I started to count, among the successional species such as black cherry, a number of red oak seedlings, probably progeny of the large red oak in my neighbor's side yard. This meadow was rapidly succeeding to forest. If I allowed these seedlings to grow and kept the invasives from shading them out or sending out toxic substances that would prevent them from thriving, I would eventually have a forest, woodland punctuated by useful lawn and a vegetable patch.

By the sixth summer I imagined that my neighbors had come to recognize my front yard reforestation and vegetable patch project as the next wave in home gardening and that they had started to grumble less. There was always a small cadre of neighbors who indulged me and patiently waited through the ugly phase, but there was also some pushback. My kids winced when I suggested that they have friends over. "Our house looks a mess," they would say. True, compared with the tidy front yards of some of their classmates, our house did indeed look a mess, if not outright abandoned. A friend commented that all I needed to do was to set an old refrigerator and rotting couch out on the front porch to complete the look he described, in his Alabama accent, as "gone country." But by this time I was kind of hooked. I wanted to see what would happen if I just let the landscape do what it wanted to do and then managed it, coppicing, pruning, occasionally weeding, adding plants here and there.

What happened sometimes seemed incredible. After the first couple of years of coppicing the black cherry seedlings, I found cherry seedlings popping up with lighter bark and small, pink blooms: ornamental cherries. After a year or two of pruning them up to encourage them to be the specimen trees they were probably originally cultivated to be, I noticed that one along the driveway, right at the curb, had started to lean awkwardly toward the road. Pruning was a problem. By the end of the summer, however, the leaves had begun to cascade down toward the ground. Not only was this not a black cherry, it was no regular ornamental cherry but a weeping cherry. This was when the concept of horticultural karma came to me. When I had done residential work years before and had completed what I thought was a stunning yet understated, elegant design, clients occasionally would say the same thing: "Okay, all good. But where do I put my weeping cherry?" It seemed that a weeping cherry was the specimen flavor of the year, and I dreaded that question. So now, years later, the universe had sent me my very own weeping

The "weeds" included a weeping cherry, which the author underplanted with fall asters.

cherry, in the place of honor, right at the arrival to my house. And I learned to love my weeping cherry, to underplant it with euphorbias and fall asters.

Letting Things Happen . . . to a Point

I was not completely surprised when, arriving home one afternoon that sixth summer, I recognized the telltale slip of white paper inserted into my screen door: a summons. A Licenses and Inspection officer must have visited my little plot, for I was cited for violating section 8.4 of the Philadelphia building code, allowing "weeds greater than 10 inches tall, bushes," to grow unchecked in my front yard. I looked at the wild front landscape and then at the vegetable patch; the tomatoes were growing well over 10 inches, as was the rhubarb. Was I being cited for my vegetables or my "weeds"? Does an L&I inspector actually know the difference? Probably an irritated neighbor had called in the city; was it the front yard farm or the weeds that most offended?

I called to get my hearing scheduled in March of the next year. Apparently there are a lot of citations for weeds, or other similar matters, regularly landing in the weed judge's docket. I would argue my case and, I was certain, win. Yet something troubled me. My neighbors, my children, and now the city had a lot of trouble appreciating my wild experiment. What was I trying to prove? Might there be some sort of compromise, so that I could reside somewhere within spitting distance of the normal and not remain an outlaw? My experiment was for my own edification and pleasure; if it caused those around me true discomfort, wasn't that a bad ecological move? To maintain order in my house and on my block I needed to spruce up my landscape. I needed help.

I had had landscapers come look before, but somehow when I told them I didn't want to clean the entire place up, they were too busy or never called back. But this time, after many calls to friends for referrals, I found

The front vegetable patch, year 8.

Roddy von Seldeneck, a former New York University film student, who had dropped out to follow his passion for horticulture and landscaping. Roddy seemed not only up to the task but interested. He showed up with his crew, they started to weed-whack and prune back the seedlings, and they mowed and edged the lawn strips. My landscape went from just plain rough to tidily rough-and-tumble. We began an interesting partnership: Roddy understood that I needed him only for big jobs and emergencies, and I understood that he had free rein when it came to pruning and transplanting. But our partnership arrangement did not come easily; it took one major conflagration to gel.

Not Freaking Out

The first November after Roddy started working on my landscape, he met me one morning to go over the tasks for the day. I asked him to mulch the vegetable patch with the leaf mold that had been heating up in my leaf pile over the past several years and to clean up a lot of debris from the fall. I left for work, and when I came back not only was the rectangular vegetable patch neatly patted down with that dark, rich humus, but the entire front woodland had been weed-whacked and mulched. True, it was home-grown dark mulch, which would turn down into the soils easily by late spring, but it was mulch nevertheless. What had looked like a meadow now looked like a mulch-field. Roddy learned that day what my reaction to such dramatic and unforeseen changes to the plan could be: I totally freaked out.

"I can't have a front yard full of mulch," I told Roddy.

He explained that what they took out was mostly stilt-grass, an invasive grasslike species that indeed had been advancing through my small lot at an alarming rate. I couldn't argue with that. I looked around at the shallow layer of leaf mold and saw a few violet leaves already beginning to show through. This was the right thing to do. But I asked him to underplant that very day, with woodland perennials, so it wouldn't look like a suburban mulch-and-gravel garden with weedy trees growing up through it.

I gave Roddy a budget of $200 to go find whatever he could that would live there, and he came back with hellebores, anemones, and ferns. By that afternoon I had a nascent woodland garden, with a lot of mulch showing, but the neighbors all commented on how nice it looked, and I thanked Roddy, I told him I would try never to freak out again, and he and his guys put the landscape to bed for the winter.

The messy front yard officially became a wild garden after Anne Raver wrote about it in the *New York Times*.

The high and dry side garden along the driveway became the place for experimenting with herbs, annuals, and yuccas, the plant of choice for the no-go medians at Queens Plaza.

The next spring, after I successfully argued my case with the weed judge, armed with photographs and botanical names, the woodland garden made a glorious if youthful showing. I started to spend more time in the vegetable patch, planting sulphur cosmos and zinnias and bright-red dahlias as well as collards and tomatoes. The neighbors seemed to smile more, and when Anne Raver, the journalist who has written about projects I have worked on and is one of the most progressive writers and gardeners I know, came to write about the summons story and what a wild garden might be, the small cadre of neighbors who had indulged me all along gave great quotes about how they had wondered what I was doing but trusted that I was following some plan. They gave me way more credit for foresight than I ever had.

And suddenly, after years of being known for public projects in the sustainable vein, I began popping up around the Internet as a wild gardener. I had never liked being considered green or a proponent of sustainable design. My former partner, Judith Heintz, and I began to design projects in the early 1990s that reused materials and promoted a rougher look because as young women competing for jobs, we won projects with miserably small budgets, and we were just making do. But we liked the ethic involved, plus the design and technical challenges. We never aimed to be "sustainable designers," just good designers. So when I was added to teams to provide the green component, I squirmed. I was asked to give talks and write articles, but the role of sustainability expert seemed a stretch. We were all doing the same things; most landscape architects and designers were shifting practices of stormwater management and construction methods to be less wasteful, to enhance habitat, to integrate wildlife habitat, and I certainly wasn't a lone pioneer.

Many of us had grown leery of the sustainability focus in landscape, watching it become a formula, resulting in responsible and handsome projects with bioswales and green roofs, all of which definitely contribute to our ecological health. What about the other items we need to sustain life, such as connection to other people, or cultural expression? Green developed as a series of checklists that reduced design to the adoption of "best practices," but what about design?

Avoiding Labels

The modern minimalist style of architecture that just happened to coincide with sustainability became naturalized as the preeminent language of green: long, linear bioswales, long, linear benches without backs, long, linear pavers. At first, these projects seemed like a radical departure from previous conventions of landscape design, which had become elaborate and sometimes overdesigned in the hyped-up postmodernism of the 1980s and 1990s. But by the time sustainability had moved from a fringe preoccupation into the mainstream of practice, the most frequently published and talked-about landscape projects started to look more and more the same and, oddly, lifeless. For some reason this was almost considered a rational design method—rational because it performed.

Challenging the Idea That Design Is Rational

Rather than completely cutting down a silver maple that died in year 2, the author left 15 feet of a double trunk. It has become home for many insects, which attract woodpeckers, and a bat box was mounted on the south-facing side of the tree.

Landscape designers made green parking lots, with lushly planted bioswales instead of those sorry lawn-and-tree medians, but we as a culture were still addicted to driving and shopping. TV shows on "green living" started to pop up, with green versions of "Cribs" that featured 25,000-square-foot houses with photovoltaic cells, geothermal energy, or wastewater recycling. No matter how "green" you design it, a 25,000-square-foot house is just not sustainable. You can design the most responsible and low-impact landscape in the world, but if we are still building big and not changing our habits, we are still screwed. It was at this time, when I was developing a reputation that made me cringe, that I began to ask the question, "What are we doing here, anyway?" It is a question that has resonated with people far and wide. It seems that many people were asking themselves the same question: What are the deeper values that we are trying to uphold and nurture? If we are designing everything to be biodegradable and zero-carbon and low-embodied energy but we are spending our leisure time doing parallel play on our laptops, what are we doing here, anyway?

We were not asking these questions as judgment of other people's behaviors. I myself was far from living a green life, driving too much and using bleach-based products and chemically toxic flea treatments for my dog, traces of which can now be found in the groundwater. I have never insulated my attic—my interior renovation was way more important at the time than energy efficiency—and every winter I discover another little sliver of air under a door or around a window that I have not stopped up with a strip of putty. I fly in airplanes, a lot of them, to go work on projects around the world that are known for being ecologically oriented. Okay, I thought, we are all "designing green," but unless we completely change the way we live, the landscape as we know it is not going to survive. Much as my profession might spend its time trying to make beautiful places for people to connect with nature and each other, we are still totally steeped in the culture of consumerism, held back by our own bad habits.

Tapping into What Is Wild

So now that my landscape has been branded a wild garden, I have started to make the connection between being wild and delving deeper into what it means to be environmentally oriented. I am starting to believe that there is something about how unruly our process is, how rich and full of life our landscapes can be, that points us toward environmental health. It has less to do with thinking about best practices in our heads than with experiencing wildness on a physical level. Embracing the wild is a way of life, not just our duty as landscape stewards; we thrill to a proliferation of pokeweed in our gardens not because of the Leadership in Energy and Environmental Design points it might earn us but because it is beautiful, and alive, and has medicinal value. It is the messy undergrowth beneath the trees that allows life to thrive; life happens in the places you do not keep well manicured and chemically treated. This is as true in parks as it is in my own garden.

One event that has brought home to me the mysterious dynamic that engages natural processes and human thoughts and actions involved milkweed. Milkweed has a particular place in my own history because I grew up in a New York City apartment, and in the late fall we would every once in a while look up to see strange, ephemeral-looking white filaments floating through the air. I only learned what they were when I was around 12, on a Thanksgiving drive with the family, and I saw one of the strange dried stalks topped by a rough-textured pod bursting with some sort of foamy, silky substance. Pulling at it, I discovered that the white filaments separated easily, that in fact these held the seeds, and these were the strange wisps that floated through our apartment periodically. I learned much later how important milkweed is to monarch butterflies in particular, and that its population has been reduced drastically by development and by farmers eradicating it as a weed. When I moved to the little ranch house in Philadelphia I was so excited to find milkweed growing at the end of the driveway, on the high and dry bank. Around the sixth year, a year when I was particularly busy and didn't plant tomatoes to grow up the wire frames in the garden, I found milkweed colonizing the vegetable patch. Odd, given how good the soils were, and how shady the edge of the garden where they showed up was. Maybe another instance of horticultural karma.

What are the measurable effects of designing wild landscapes, beyond just being appealing to people like me? There are three key perceived benefits to making wild landscapes. One is obviously the habitat they provide for species other than humans. Another is the benefit to humans in terms of health and wellness. And the third is a benefit to humans and wildlife: the way in which wild landscapes promote stewardship.

Milkweed colonizing the vegetable patch.

These Wissahickon schist boulders were unearthed when the high, dry side garden next to the driveway was dug out. Not knowing what she wanted to do with them, the author asked landscaper Roddy von Seldeneck and crew to put them on the concrete pad in the back garden, which she had always disliked. A crack in the concrete ensued: she let this green "weed river" grow in the crack but pulls out invasives such as mugwort.

HABITAT This book operates under the assumption that it is good to create habitat for wildlife. We believe that it's important to try to increase the planet's biodiversity and try to stave off the mass extinctions that are occurring under our watch. But some scientists argue that we are too far gone for our efforts to make much of a difference. There is not a whole lot of evidence to support the belief that designers can actually make a dent in the downward spiral of the planet's ecosystems. And some believe that this downward spiral is "natural"—that this sixth extinction is as inevitable as the dramatic event, still perhaps a mystery, that killed off the dinosaurs—and that the planet will survive and reconfigure itself, as it has in the previous five extinctions. So apart from the conservation conceit, what is important about creating habitat? Faced with the question of whether habitat restoration and conservation are all vanity, it's possible that we create habitat in our projects just because we can, because it is a beautiful process and there is something that compels us to promote life. Why have children? With all the evidence that we are heading into terrible times in which water and food will be contested terrain, why create more people? Because we can, and because it is an instinct and a drive. Once you get into the habit of making projects that are full of life, it is difficult to go back to the more sterile forms of practice.

HEALTH Then there is the more obviously selfish goal of promoting human health and wellness. Richard Louv's book *Last Child in the Woods* argues that contemporary children, disconnected from nature, experience far higher degrees of attention deficit disorder, hyperactivity, obesity, and depression. He produces much empirical evidence that supports the idea that connection to nature, just being outside, significantly mitigates these problems. Gardening may be so popular the world over not just to produce food or flowers but because the soil contains antidepressant substances; working in the earth makes you feel better. The connection between being in nature and health has been researched and written about by E. O. Wilson, Wendell Berry, Howard Frumkin, Richard Jackson, and myriad others. The Norwegian tradition of *friluftsliv*, or "open air living," has been seized on by people around the globe as a model for how we can connect with nature in our daily lives.

STEWARDSHIP The third reason to create landscapes that immerse people in environments that support many forms of life is that connecting with nature helps people to feel invested, to want to take care. The best place to start promoting stewardship is in designing for children.

In the remaining chapters I lay out what I have come to understand as the operations—what we are really doing—in making beautiful landscapes that reconnect people with larger natural systems, whether it is by enhancing wildlife habitat or creating a garden in the city that makes you feel like you are in a fern canyon.

Approaching Design Strategically

There are many different ways of creating change in the landscape, all of them having an impact on the larger structure of the environment, as the story of my own yard transformation shows. Asking the hard questions about what we are doing in any given phase of a project can help us understand that we have many different tools, many different strategies, to do our work. We are not only asking ourselves what practice are we deploying—are we operating at the planning scale, are we engaged in form-making, are we enhancing the ecosystems of the site—but we are digging deep to find out what the nature of our transformative work really is. By naming the strategies we use, we can define who we are on this particular project or for this particular task. We can focus on the different forms of analysis we need to do, the different tools we will need to use, the different types of drawing we will need to do.

The Wildlife Federation and the Audubon Society as well as many local nature societies offer back yard wildlife habitat certification. The requirements are that the property provide food, shelter, and water. The old food oil vats, having been empty of oil for decades and cleaned extensively, fulfill the water part.

The silver maple snag stands above a pokeweed garden. All the growth was promoted by one act: stopping mowing.

The next five chapters of this book outline the five main strategies I find myself using continually, over the range of projects that come my way. This list—Reinvention, Restoration, Conservation, Regeneration, and Expression— is not meant to be comprehensive for every designer. These are simply the key strategies I have found myself pursuing in my own work, work undertaken with a large number of collaborators. I encourage readers to come up with their own list of strategies and to name them differently. Designers and planners are as unique as the landscapes we work in, and their methods and outcomes should, more often than not, differ in a way that makes all our disciplines as rich and deep as a terminal moraine.

We start our planning and design work long before we actually draw anything. From the moment we receive a site map or site photos, or even as soon as we hear of a project, we begin thinking about what the site is, what it's going to become. We know that we could transform the site in many significant ways, and often design solutions have percolated up into our consciousness

before we have even signed a contract. Yet as designers we are rarely conscious of all the different strategies we deploy, the different planning and design processes, and the different scales at which we need to respond, from project to project and even from task to task within a project.

Liberty State Park Interior, a successional landscape with an overlay of new program and wetland restoration, needed a clear system of access. The strategy was to use the old rail lines, the path of water flow, and the successional movement of plant species across the site to organize circulation.

The language in a request for proposals or a project brief can be very revealing. "A derelict waterfront site," for instance, lets us know that the site is considered degraded, in need of a major transformation; "an ecologically fragile valley," on the other hand, probably describes a place that needs to be conserved, safeguarded from the damage we could do inserting new uses, new programs, into the site, or from growing development surrounding it. "A 1980s corporate atrium that has become dated" may call only for some cosmetic work, noninvasive injectables such as new plantings, or resurfacing with new pavers.

We do our work on many different levels, in many different roles: We plan the big moves, develop new programs for the way a site will be used, and draw plans from the scale of a city to the scale of a garden to the scale of a planting bed.

Designing the Design Process

Understanding all the different functions we take on as designers can help us craft the design and planning processes themselves. Doing this allows us to structure our work, to choose our tools carefully, and to pace ourselves. Once we become conscious of what we are doing (is it planning, is it design, ecology? are we completely reinventing the site, or are we restoring what has been lost?), we grasp how little time most of us will spend on physical, formal design over the life of a project. A lot of our work will involve lists and phone calls and e-mails and meetings, plenty of diagrams, but very little time sitting at our desks "designing."

Thus, the strategies in this book can be applied in a variety of ways: to our planning, to our "nondesign work," and to the sites themselves. Rather than approach the "nondesign" aspects of our work as less important, we learn that we can mobilize all our creative powers behind every task, not just the manipulation of form. The diagrams we do while in the planning phase of a project can have a greater impact than a host of lovely Photoshop renderings. A well-conceived diagram can give direction to the design team and can hold them to the larger conceptual framework of a project.

I use these strategies to guide my work, aiming to create projects that grow out of the site, that are transformative, that safeguard the natural world, that leave the site at least as healthy as we found it (if not better), that set processes in motion to ensure the health of the landscape and community long after we are gone, that express something beyond just what it is, that can stand alone as an expressive art.

REINVENTION Almost every project we take on has an element of reinvention: We are called in to make some change to the landscape that will bring it closer to the vision, or the need, the client expresses to us. For this reason, I start out with the chapter "Reinvention" to emphasize that every time we enter into the design process, even with the most small-scale intervention, we are reinventing the site. But some projects more than others call out not for a makeover but rather a complete redo—a heart transplant, say, instead of simply cleaning out the arteries.

RESTORATION Other projects call for a subtle realignment of the site, a chiropractic approach, restoring flow and health to the landscape. These projects are more about restoration of certain site components—structures, relation-ships, habitats. The heavy lifting in these projects is not creating a whole new world but bringing the existing world back into a healthy whole, restoring the systems and structures that were lost over years or, sadly, during the process of construction. Soils need to be reestablished, slopes revegetated, healthy flow of water reestablished. Sometimes the process of restoration is effected in a single move, such as reconnecting a city and the river from which it was cut off by a highway, in a particularly traumatic habit of the last century.

CONSERVATION Some projects require a cautious, walking-on-eggshells approach to safeguard something precious within the site, whether it is a diverse tropical forest or the people who have lived on the site for centuries. These are the projects where the site is so compelling and attractive—2,500 acres in the Western Ghats of India, for instance—that a developer, a govern-ment agency, or an institution decides to capitalize on the attraction. But the introduction of new buildings and programs could possibly destroy whatever precious landscape is there. In many of our projects, our most powerful move can be the line in the sand, saying that nothing is to be built in the forest reserve, for instance. Many countries now have regulations and restrictions to prevent loss of such natural resources, but enforcement is not always assured, so designing our own regulatory and restrictive sanctions within a project can ensure that boundaries will not be crossed nor regulations violated.

Our work has fewer standards when it comes to conserving cultural and human resources. Introducing new buildings and programs can often dev-astate local economies and compromise an area's cultural resources. In her influential book *Staying Alive*, Vandana Shiva describes the intricate econo-mies, many almost invisible to outsiders, that sustain areas where aid funding focuses on large infrastructure projects. She details the ways in which large projects often unwittingly destroy local cultures and economies. It is essential not only to observe these resources, to study and understand how they oper-ate, but to engage and partner with the people who steward them.

REGENERATION Some projects require that we set up systems that will begin to revive and regenerate the site in a process that may continue for many years. This process can be set in motion by an economic catalyst, such as an income-generating program that can bring new life to a site. The regen-erative device might be an ecological program to set a process of revegetation in motion. Regeneration has to be understood as a process that will be set in motion and continue to occur long after the designer's role in the project has ended. Models and modes of representation that illustrate what will happen in 5, 10, 20, 50 years are often needed for such projects.

EXPRESSION Finally, there are the most obviously artistic projects that tap into creative veins deep inside us, and draw on a perceived or projected nature of the site, to express who we are and where we live. There are a million definitions of what art is. Rather than trying to come up with a description of how landscape design can inhabit the realm of art, I will look only at how certain landscape projects express an emotion or an idea—what it feels like to be in a fern canyon in Oregon, or how marine life can be expressed in architectural form and technological means. But really good artists do not just express an idea using whatever methods happen to come to mind. They often ask a question, and then give themselves a set of rules to follow, and then follow that process, seeing where it takes them, filtering the results through a highly critical eye, or ear, or whatever sense the art form appeals to.

I hope readers do not take away from this classification the idea that any given project will use one strategy and one strategy alone. There are elements of all strategies in many projects. My goal in classifying the strategies is simply to bring attention to what the governing strategy is in a project or a task. It's comparable to the Zen practice of stopping and asking, "What is it?" You may think you are "designing," but in fact if you keep your attention in the present, fixed on the specifics of what you are doing, you can properly organize your work, assemble your tools, prepare and collaborate with the right team members, and work at the optimal scale to achieve what you want to achieve. It is shocking how often we are not mindful of what scale we really should be working at.

My goal in the following chapters is to call out the different strategies but also to encourage easy flow from one to another. Finally, I hope there can be an element of expression in every project we undertake. By leaving this strategy for last, I hope to encourage readers to bring the art part—the joy of making something beautiful (understanding the slipperiness of this term from Toru Mitani's comments about power lines), and of living with it—into every endeavor they undertake. And this is part of my own adventure in sustainability, discovering that beauty and joy not only are desirable but often are the secret ingredients in making projects truly sustainable.

Queens Plaza
reinvented, just after
construction.

Chapter 2:

Reinvention

There are sites you walk onto for the first visit and think to yourself, "This place is gorgeous, I am so lucky to have a job like this, and what can I do to avoid messing it up?" Then there are sites where you have to spend some time looking around, you think it's a great place but there are things that are a little amiss, you have to squint a little to see the overall form of things, and you think, "Hmm, if I just move this over there, and regrade that, and screen that, and provide a better sense of arrival, this place will be amazing." You feel lucky in this case, too, to work with such a great, if flawed, site and to have been trained with a combination of creativity and pragmatism to know how to fix it.

Then there are the sites you walk onto, look around, and think, "Oh my God, this place is a disaster." But whether it is dangerous or polluted, or nothing works, or it's an eyesore with acres of broken pavement—there are few cases when you actually think you've landed a bad project and you don't want to do it. If I can reinvent this place, building on what it is but completely changing the way it is perceived and the way it functions, this could be a fantastic place.

Reinvention does not rely on one tactic alone; the actions can range from modest, something that might take a week, to monumental, a project that can take 12 years. Here, not in order of magnitude, are some of the ways we can reinvent a place:

Cleaning up: Sometimes the most effective action we can take is the smallest. Just cleaning the trash from the sidewalks and gutters and painting facades can completely transform a run-down street, as has been seen on Germantown Avenue in Philadelphia. The street is not just cleaned up, it is reinvented as a place that people tend to and care about. The amount of littering, graffiti, and even violent crime generally decreases when a street or neighborhood has simply been cleaned up. The most ambitious project to redesign a street will fall flat if people still throw their trash on the ground.

Reframing: Quite often the brief we are given—whether it is the contract limit line, or the program, or even the nominal client—does not, on analysis, turn out to adhere to reality. The line around the project does not take into account adjacent property that could add value to the project, or take value away if it ended up in the wrong hands. The program may not be feasible; often the wish list could be accommodated only in a site many times as large as the site at hand. So when we begin a project we need to reframe the question, and the givens, to ask ourselves whether the limits of the project are adequate, the program we are given makes sense, and the process as laid out in the brief is optimal. We need to reframe the way a place is conceived of; only after we have challenged the givens can we really get down to business.

Deconstructing: We have to understand what part of the site we need to take apart completely. Often it is the groundplane: the road system, or parking lots, or lawn. In reinventing sites we are sometimes like surgeons, taking whole parts of the body apart but leaving enough intact to keep the patient alive.

Rewiring: We also can change the many flows of a place: the flow of people, the flow of water, the flow of air even. We can design a fantastic landscape, but unless we have analyzed the flows of energy and figured out how to reroute them to make the place work as well as it can, we can easily fail.

Transforming: If they detract from the experience of the place, the parts of the landscape that we are not taking apart completely, or rewiring, can be transformed by means that range from minimal to monumental. Just painting an elevated rail line, for example, can transform the place tremendously, but we can also clad it anew, light it up, add structure to it. We have to know which parts of a project we can transform, and how.

Constructed wetland below,
elevated subway above,
Queens Plaza.

Reprogramming: How people use a place has as much to do with the way a particular landscape looks and feels as the most obvious formal design. Just adding a new program, or eliminating unwanted uses, can be as dramatic a reinvention as a complete physical overhaul.

Cleaning Up Messes

Projects that require reinvention can be compelling and challenging, and once you start working on them you can get hooked. Few of us can afford to turn projects down, but many of us simply love a challenge, a mess to tidy up. Bette Midler once said that she started the New York Restoration Project because she saw all the garbage on the side of the highways and she likes to clean things up; she said she wanted "to get the trash off the street and onto the stage, where it belongs."

Queens Plaza, Long Island City, New York City

A lot of us are driven by the urge to fix damaged things, make broken things work, if not actually heal the landscape. Queens Plaza was such a site: When you walked up Queens Boulevard in the shadow of the elevated trains and saw just swirling acres of roadway and crazy traffic making crazy turns and people running for their lives to get across the street, there was no way you could think, "If we just do a little bit of this and move around a little bit of that, this place will be okay." You had to stand there and suspend your belief in everything you were seeing. You had to invent a process of study and work that would lead you to an understanding of the less visible integrities of the site that you could build on, and then to maybe a series of alternative schemes that would each provide a strong theme for the landscape. For such a major transformation it's good to test a few ideas, ideas strong enough to stand up to the noxious qualities of the place, because you can't prejudge what will work. And if you were just to fix this and move that, the place would still be a disaster. You have to dismantle the place as it exists. You have to reinvent what it is. You have to say, "This place once was a tangled, prohibitive mess, but it is going to be a park, a gateway, and a beautiful link between two boroughs." Once you are done, people will move beyond what it was, and it will become something other. Retaining much of the existing site doesn't actually retain the character of the place. Almost everything—the way the place looks and feels, the way it works—will be different.

In reinventing a site sometimes it is helpful to stop looking. Once you have filled up on a tremendous amount of visual information you can feel flooded. It helps to close your eyes and process what you have taken in. Quite often you can conjure up what the place might be like, how it could be reinvented.

There are sites, occasionally, where much as you squint and study and work hard, they will never be reinvented. A landfill, for instance. There is something about the engineered shape of a landfill that will always read as a big pile, maybe a big pile with beautiful successional plantings and paths and gardens. But because you can't change the topography—the cap on the garbage must be kept inviolate—the paths often feel awkward, and the slopes are too steep and too regular to be anything else.

What we do when we reinvent a project is that we create—we fabricate—a whole, believable world. There is a range of scales at which we work when we reinvent a site: We can bulldoze much of it under, or we can turn a hulking structure into a light sculpture just with the use of fixtures. Queens Plaza probably sits at the more comprehensive reinvention end of the spectrum, retaining the larger infrastructure, but with a redesigned roadway system and a new green matrix of plantings and new pavements and medians, becoming a completely new place.

For many decades, Queens Plaza, where the borough of Queens' major thoroughfare stops just short of Manhattan, at the East River, was considered a terrible place. A tangle of elevated trains and bridges, it spread out in a chaotic sea of roadbeds and parking lots, run through by a depressed business corridor. Among the few businesses to thrive were a number of gentlemen's clubs, supported by both the sex and drug trades that found a haven in Queens Plaza. To top it off, when prisoners were released from Rikers Island they were dropped off at Queens Plaza, under the elevated, in the middle of the night, with several dollars to get them wherever they were going.

Starting in the late 1990s, the New York Department of City Planning and several nonprofits launched an effort to transform Queens Plaza—to make it less dangerous, more welcoming, and to attract businesses to the area. An ideas competition run in 2001 by the Van Alen Institute yielded a number of compelling visions for the area that built on, rather than tried to mask, the imposing infrastructure.

In 2003, building on the enthusiasm that the ideas competition sparked for reclaiming Queens Plaza as a positive civic space, the New York City Department of City Planning launched the Queens Plaza Pedestrian and

Originally, the Queensboro Bridge alighted onto a grand civic square in Long Island City, c. 1910.

By 2003 Queens Plaza could no longer be navigated safely.

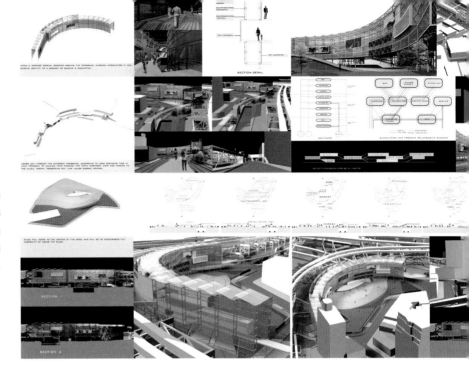

The winning submission in the Van Alen Institute's 2003 competition to reenvision Queens Plaza, by Surachai Akekapobyotin and Jutha-thip Techachumreon.

Bicycle Improvement Project. The goal of the project was to humanize the massive swath of concrete and metal—the broad roadbeds, the elevated train tracks, the bridge itself. The project also sought to mitigate the noise and pollution from traffic on and off the Queensboro Bridge and the sound of the elevated trains as they whirled around Queens Plaza, a sound that had come to be known as "the screech." My team submitted a proposal and won the project with an urban designer, a civil engineer, an artist, a lighting designer, an environmental engineer, and a number of subconsultants.

Designing the Design Process

Design does not just happen. The process must be carefully orchestrated, giving everyone involved enough time and enough attention to do what they have been trained to do better than others. Big, complex urban infrastructure projects call for big teams, which is sometimes a good thing and at other times not so good a thing. The good part is the multiple levels of expertise and the potential for a collaborative outcome to be greater than the sum of its parts; the bad part is that big teams are challenging to manage. In terms of process, it helps to have a detailed, clear scope for each team member and a schedule saying when they will go to meetings, what work they will be responsible for; otherwise, consultants can do work that is unnecessary and run through fees very quickly. More importantly, however, a big team can fall short when it comes to a transformative vision for reinventing a site. There must be one strong lead who can push the vision through the design-by-committee pit-falls of teamwork, prioritizing efforts so that the pragmatic concerns do not sink the transformative vision, nor does the vision promise something that cannot be manifested in reality. The process is not linear: With so many moving parts, not only the many challenging existing conditions but the many agencies, community groups, and approval bodies, the sequence of meetings and working sessions can seem to be more of a round robin than a straight path. The design process must keep the team circling back to the vision and the big gestures; otherwise, it can devolve into problem solving only, or the team can lose its focus on the larger goals as it tries to answer to the many desires and concerns of the many stakeholders.

Reinventing Infrastructure

The 1-mile corridor of Queens Boulevard that runs from the Sunnyside Yards in Long Island City to the East River has traditionally been not only inhospitable but dangerous. Crossing the many lanes of traffic, some of which took unpredictable curving turns up onto the Queensboro Bridge, could be deadly, as a number of traffic deaths over the years proved. It was difficult to find your way from north to south, bridging the two low-density

Queens Plaza 2003. This was where Rikers Island prisoners were dropped off in the middle of the night when they were released. Crossing the street and traffic was so perilous, this stretch of the street was nicknamed "The Boulevard of Death."

neighborhoods on each side. Bicyclists could hardly find their way through this morass of metal and asphalt.

The new landscape had to reinvent Queens Plaza as a place where it's easy to find the way to the subway or the bus, where people are happy riding their bikes from home to work, and where the industrial character of Long Island City is retained but the neighborhood made more livable. The new landscape also had to change Queens Plaza from gray to green, reinventing it as a desirable civic landscape.

Transforming the Everyday

In order to reinvent a site, it's sometimes helpful to step away from the photo-reality of the place and make something radically different. You can deconstruct the place and then see how you can put it back together in a new way. This diagram from 2003 acted as a visual prompt for the team's goals: to transform the space into a place where the infrastructure and landscape work together, where connections are made and energy generated, a place with plants and light and water.

Once our team had pulled this vision of Queens Plaza together and we started to develop a concept, we came up with three alternative approaches to the project: the green ribbon scheme, which would capitalize on the water flowing down the street toward the East River to cultivate lush plantings; the urban beach scheme, less focused on plantings and more on generating lively patterns on the paved surfaces and on treating the overhead structures as opportunities for entertainment, with media walls and light displays; and the urban forest scheme, which filled the open spaces with grids of trees, or large bosques, as they are called. The client and team inclined toward the green ribbon idea because it was the most green, drawing on best practices of sustainable design, and at that time sustainability was at the foreground of the field. Ten years later, the field of landscape architecture has so internalized best practices that a scheme built entirely on sustainability would not be as appealing or interesting.

In building the team, we needed to find an urban design and architecture practice that would be able to collaborate on all aspects of the project, because there was so much overlap between bridges and elevated and roadway and medians. In 2004 we had a change in team composition, and we needed to interview a new urban designer or architect. I wondered how to interview designers to take on this complex project. We put together the diagram at right, which described the goals of the project in a visual language.

Thinking on Many Levels

To imagine a reinvention of Queens Plaza we needed to think on many levels at once. This diagram shows how components of the landscape operate in multiple capacities: a metal scrim acts as signage, as visual noise abatement, and as a solar collector. The project called for the designers to build on a complex existing infrastructure. We needed to find an urban design firm that would embrace the elevated.

I interviewed three of the leading urban design and architecture firms in the city. All three did some studies that would have served the project well. One firm talked in the interview about how they would develop several iconic objects within the triangular park, to provide identity and add life to the street. Another firm went back to our original design concept, organizing the streetscape into one very bold landscape running east and west. Both of these responses were smart, clear, and appealing. The third firm, Marpillero Pollak (MPA), focused on the need for serious study of all the elevated rail and bridge structures, without saying where this study would take them, or us. This type of "I don't know" response often does not do well when a client wants to know exactly what they will be getting as a product. But for such a complex project, we respected MPA's candor in not being able predict what the solution might be.

The three responses from the different urban designers roughly parallel three key methods you can adopt in making significant change to the landscape. First there is the icon landscape, such as Millennium Park. It is the objects—the Frank Gehry band shell, the Anish Kapoor mirrored sculpture, and the fountain-spewing faces—that give this park its identity. Then there is the overlay, as in Arlington National Cemetery, where a grid is overlaid on a naturalistic landform or topography. The third method is a more organic process: The forms of the design emerge from studying the existing conditions and working together as a team, so that, for instance, the environmental engineer's work on winds starts to influence the shapes and flows on the site. There are times, however, when the first or second approach is preferable. At Queens Plaza we adopted the third, the slow and steady let's-see-where-it-will-take-us method.

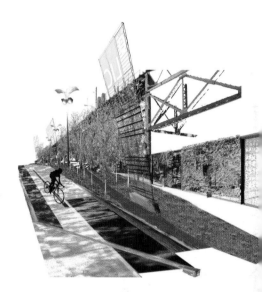

Taking the vision into a visual language that conveys water flow, infrastructure greening, and noise abatement.

We interviewed each team at their office. It wasn't until the principals of MPA invited us for a coffee in the three-story living space at the back of their office that we started to appreciate what they would add to the process. What we saw made us understand that MPA were in the business of reinvention, whether it was at the scale of the city, or a loft, or a small garden. They had opened the entire back half of the building both down, into the basement level, and up, to the second floor. Three stories of building—a building within a loft—created a stacked space, with a mezzanine bedroom, a ground floor bedroom, and then a raw-beam staircase, no railing, leading down into the living space below. The entire space looked out onto a shallow, surrealistic garden of gravel with low plantings nestled at the edges, water flowing from cut stones, and mirrors placed in a grid along the back garden wall. Connecting the spaces were catwalks supported by the leftover beams taken down to open the space up. The design retained a strong sense of what it had been—the brick, many structural frameworks left intact even when no longer necessary, for example—but also created a whole new world, in fact a stacked apartment within a loft, almost a little city. For MPA the process of reinvention did not involve sanitizing the existing architecture to make it all perfect, nor was their approach to the old particularly deferential or polite, for they took it apart and reassembled it with a kind of muscularity that was quite dramatic.

I was impressed not only by how ingeniously MPA had reused so much of what they had found in demolition but also by how they had assembled and sculpted a glamorous but comfortable world that felt connected to its history. Their ability to take what was there, transform it with powerful gestures, but also retain the spirit of what it once was got them the job. Queens Plaza needed someone who would be able to deconstruct the place and then reconfigure it with nothing short of love. MPA won one of the most visible urban design jobs in the city at the time on the basis of the ingenious reinvention of their loft, not simply their professional portfolio. And in the design process they prepared voluminous studies of the elevated, looking for patterns and rhythms, relating these to the flow of pedestrian traffic, the crosswalks, and the desired routes through the site. Their studies helped reinvent the way people move through the site, the way people perceive of the place, the way the place functions on every level.

Reinventing Flows: Water

The reinvention of Queens Plaza does not eliminate or screen or seek to obscure the massive infrastructure of roadway and elevated. The design takes the forces at work, such as stormwater pouring down from the bridges, for example, and turns them into something positive. Before the transformation, during rains the water flowing off the bridge dumped directly onto the sidewalks and streets, sometimes from more than 50 feet above pedestrians' heads. Now the stormwater runs through median plantings that slow it down, cleansing it as it makes its way down to the river.

The design of the medians integrates the flow of water through the site but goes beyond mere utility: The design establishes an aesthetic of movement and flow that is expressive of the forces at work at Queens Plaza. The flow of people and the flow of vegetation cultivated by on-site water meld with the flow of traffic (and the accompanying DOT graphics) to create an environment in which all these elements can coexist.

The graphic language of traffic striping, a Department of Transportation design, blends with the flow of the curbs, bike lane, and furnishings to create a design that has no boundaries.

Reinventing Flows: People

The task for MPA was to transform the structure of the elevated as part of the newly reconceived landscape. They were true collaborators on the ground-plane itself, working closely with the landscape architects and also with the artist Michael Singer, whose work on the paving, curbing, and benches integrated the public art aspect into the overall design and details. Our approach was to reinvent the groundplane, which existed as a thin crust of pavement dwarfed by the giant infrastructure, by making it more robust, thicker, a matrix of plants and paving and benches that all felt substantial, rooted in the ground. The landscape needed to stand up to the elevated, to meet it in its force and presence. In this way we could reinvent how people move through the landscape, how the flows of pedestrians, bicyclists, cars, trains, buses, and trucks converge and disperse.

This rendering illustrates a vision of the groundplane and the elevated, lit from within, working together to create a new type of urban infrastructure landscape.

Left: Elevated as it is now with no "rooms."

Right: Park at night with elevated as it will be after lit scrims are added.

Thinking Overhead

MPA's work began with a tremendously rigorous study of the elevated and bridge structures. Studying the rhythms of the vertical supports and cross-beams, they discovered that there was a pattern of overhead volumes—"rooms," Marpillero called them, shown in the image at left—made by the structural members of the elevated. If they were treated as volumes, lined with metal-mesh scrims that would be lit from within, the structure would be transformed from an incoherent tangle of lines into a series of glowing lanterns. This not only improves the visual environment but provides important wayfinding, signaling to people where they can cross the street more safely from one side of the site to another. The landscape then becomes the ground over which this luminous elevated hovers.

Over the course of the project, the landscape has gone from snarled to composed, from harsh to lush, from prohibitive to inviting. It has also shifted from street to park. This would not have been possible if the New York City Department of City Planning had not advocated for a green solution. The department encouraged us to create a lush refuge at Dutch Kills Green, the 2-acre park at the top of the site. This was a radical move on their part. For decades, designers were enjoined from proposing extravagant plantings in parks for a number of reasons: Money for maintenance is scarce, and plantings of any significant height make park managers worry about crime. Managers and planners promote instead the idea of "defensible space," that is, spaces where you can survey the whole, avoiding conditions where you might be surprised by a robber, or worse, lurking behind the bushes. But Amanda Burden, then chair of the Department of City Planning, encouraged us to

create a green refuge. Her work of the past decades in New York had promoted a livable landscape, with plenty of seating and a welcoming character. We felt emboldened to create a real refuge for the city, an urban park that felt soft, immersive. The look of the landscape—somewhat wild, with irregularly planted massings of smaller understory trees and large shrubs—was not something that made many architects and designers comfortable until recent years, when the greenness of this design approach has gained currency. Design work like this frankly scared a lot of formalist architects, as well as others, who needed a very clear sense of order and abhorred anything that seemed messy, unkempt, and unwieldy. But the wild approach has gradually taken hold, and many architects are producing drawings in which the landscape is less background for their buildings, or "parsley around the pig," as some call it, a whole environment instead of window dressing, a defining framework rather than decoration.

Thinking about Scale—and Scales

One of the most underappreciated design skills is the understanding of scale. Landscape type alone does not necessarily drive scale. Whether the project is residential, urban, rural, institutional, it may not matter; what matters is how big the space feels, how it relates to what is around it. Once the scale of an existing landscape has been studied, the response can either support it or remediate it. If an existing landscape or feature, such as a large blank wall, dwarfs something like a charming city street, it may be a good idea to break down the scale; this is why lattice and arbors along blank walls became popular. On the other hand, if something in the landscape is so massive that you just can't get around it, or maybe you even find something beautiful in it, another approach is to shift the scale of the design to meet the bigness of what is already there.

The scale of the urban infrastructure at Queens Plaza required a response that could stand up to it. So even though the completed landscape on the ground looks soft and green, the landscape has an underlying organizing structure that is clear and forceful. It stretches from the infrastructure to the buildings across from it in an axial, big-boned grid. The paths are of a width that connects with the city streets. The proportion of paving to planting was studied and selected with a great amount of intention: If the paved areas were too big, the plantings would look token; if the planted areas were too big, it would not look like it was of the city.

The underlying structure of the park—paving, furnishings—is robust enough to stand up to the immense scale of the elevated.

The attention to scale ranges from the bigger decisions of layout to the smaller decisions of how to design curbs or furnishings. The relief of the artist-designed pavers, the thickness of the concrete benches, and the height and heft of the concrete and steel curbs were all designed to meet the scale of the infrastructure. If we had used more conventional paving that reads as one sheet, with furniture that appears to have been arranged on the ground, the surface of the ground would have appeared wafer-thin in contrast to all that structure around it. So we exaggerated the scale of the materials and made everything on the ground feel as if it all emerged from the earth together, in one gesture. In reinventing a place, it's essential to understand the scale of the original and be extremely intentional about the scales—from the big overall move to the width and height of a curb—in which you choose to respond.

At Queens Plaza, the scale of the ground and the plantings also needed to accept the many different programmatic functions that were to coexist: biking, walking, driving, and lounging. We needed to distinguish the different ways of moving through the site, and we used lush plantings and also a distinction in the growing conditions to make the experience of traveling along one path different from traveling along another. The siting of the large subsurface wetland through the center of the park at the east end of the site, Dutch Kills Green, solved a pragmatic problem—what to do with the stormwater on the site—but it also created a unique microclimate that looks and feels different from everything around it. Dutch Kills is a layered landscape that operates in several different ways, both on the surface and underground.

Thinking Underground

A common misconception of an urban street is that it is the base on which the city sits. Buildings, bridges, and human activity occur on top of the solid plane of the ground. The only time one penetrates below the surface is to reach another built realm: the subway or subterranean shops. The design for Queens Plaza reconceived the groundplane as a porous surface, one layer of a multilayered system. It engaged the topography to reinvent the site not as one big flat space with a lot of metal above it but as a series of spaces, created by manipulating the contours of the earth.

The use of topography to build up a site—the ubiquitous berm, for example—is widely used across the board, from home landscapes to major parks. But the use of topography to go down is less commonly deployed. This is so for many reasons, probably the most critical being that even in a desert, if you

Queens Plaza 2003,
imagining that the site
ends at the pavement.

dig a hole or trench in the earth you have to figure out where the water will go in a rain event (and they do occur in the desert). Unless there is an existing system to allow the depression to overflow during extreme rains, when the water fills the depression up faster than it can percolate into the ground, you will generate a lot of mess, the undesirable kind, on the site. On a big urban site such as Queens Plaza there was already a subsurface stormwater system that sends water via the curbside gutters into the city's wastewater system, and eventually into the rivers, for the most part preventing the streets from flooding. The question of water is central to every project we do: Where does it come from, where will it stay on the site, and where is it going? Answering these questions requires that one think sectionally, not just in plan. Reinventing a large infrastructure such as Queens Plaza means reinventing how it works, making it work better, and that means looking at every aspect of it, from overhead to underground. By tying a new subsurface wetland into an existing system, we could slow water down, allowing better groundwater recharge, and created a wet meadow along the way. The metal boardwalk and overlooks were a response to this pragmatic solution to a drainage problem. We don't just make the design and then solve the problems; often the problems generate the design, or at least add value in their solutions.

To summarize such a nonlinear design process: This landscape of pavements looks as flat as a pancake, and the infrastructure is daunting; we would like to create a more modulated topography that will increase the sense of space and create more distinction in the places to go. We want to build up: The berms planted with hornbeams can buffer the park from the roadbeds, and the raised garden of the smaller trees and shrubs can offer a more refuge-like place to go. But we also want to dig down, to slow the water down and

cleanse it before it goes back into the city's stormwater system. The solution for this could be an amenity; one feature can multitask, solving a problem and making something people will enjoy. By making the subsurface wetland another place to go—with a metal boardwalk and places to sit along the way—we created three quite distinct experiences in a small park of less than 2 acres. If we had not looked at what was underground as part of the landscape we might have missed this opportunity to create a refuge for many people.

Walkway over constructed wetland.

Multitasking

The photograph at right shows how not only the larger landscape components but also the details can multitask. The sculptural details produced by Michael Singer's studio in collaboration with the team operate on several levels at once: The curb, which keeps people from slipping over into the wetland, is also a design with texture and relief; the small gaps where the curb pieces join direct the water from the path into the wetland. It is a safety feature, it is an art object, it is a water conveyance.

These pavers were designed to be permeable in areas of less traffic; mosses and herbs grow spontaneously in these cracks. The graphic scoring and relief Singer developed relate to the industrial history of the site and provide a grooved medium in which plants take root over time.

The artist-designed curb keeps people safe; it also allows water to flow into the wetland.

Artist-designed permeable pavers.

Finding Out Who Owns What

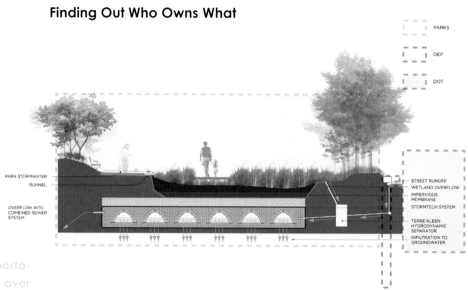

PARKS
DEP
DOT

PARK STORMWATER
RUNNEL

OVERFLOW INTO
COMBINED SEWER
SYSTEM

STREET RUNOFF
WETLAND OVERFLOW
IMPERVIOUS
MEMBRANE
STORMTECH SYSTEM

TERRE KLEEN
HYDRODYNAMIC
SEPARATOR
INFILTRATION TO
GROUNDWATER

The Department of Transportation (DOT) has jurisdiction over the streets, Department of Environmental Protection (DEP) over the gutters and sewers, and Department of Parks and Recreation (Parks) over the parkland. Coordinating maintenance of any structure that crosses the lines is difficult.

In reinventing a site, we are often taking a lot of different threads and weaving them together in a new and different way. Despite good intentions, it may be difficult to make all this work together optimally. That can be because, although the project casts the site as one site, often large urban infrastructure projects exist in many parallel realms, depending on who owns what of the site. It is rare for one body to own a whole site that involves streets and parks and elevated trains; a different agency will govern each one of these components.

The Streets Department has jurisdiction over the paths, Metropolitan Transportation Authority (MTA) over the elevated structures.

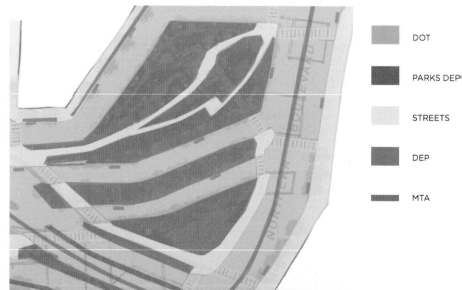

DOT

PARKS DEP

STREETS

DEP

MTA

This diagram illustrates how the subsurface wetland at Dutch Kills Green was designed to work: The water from both the park and the surrounding street was supposed to flow down into a filtration mechanism, called a hydrodynamic separator, that removes silt and debris from the stormwater before it flows into the subsurface storage and infiltration structure. However, there was one problem with this scenario, which would have resulted in the city's first public space to filter dirty stormwater from the street, returning much cleaner water into the sewer and ultimately into the city's waterways. At the time of the design, no city agency would take on the responsibility of maintaining the infamous hydrodynamic separator, which would require backing a truck up to the side of the park and vacuuming the hydrodynamic separator out, maybe once every 2 years. The real estate occupied by the filtration system fell between the cracks of several agencies, those charged with maintaining water infrastructure, maintaining parks, and maintaining city streets. So although this diagram shows street runoff flowing into the subsurface system, in fact the built design filters the stormwater only from the park site, not from the streets, leaving the dirty water in the roadbed to flow down into the conventional gutters and out into our common wastewater system, ending up, eventually, in the East River and eventually into our harbors and the ocean beyond.

PARK STORMWATER
RUNNEL

OVERFLOW INTO
COMBINED SEWER
SYSTEM

STREET RUNOFF
WETLAND OVERFLOW
IMPERVIOUS
MEMBRANE
STORMTECH SYSTEM

TERRE KLEEN
HYDRODYNAMIC
SEPARATOR
INFILTRATION TO
GROUNDWATER

Coordination between the agencies with jurisdiction over the different site components would have resulted in the dirty water from the streets being filtered within the park site.

Queens Plaza was one of the first pilot projects to test New York City's new High Performance Infrastructure Guidelines, the green guidelines intended to make the city's landscapes and buildings more sustainable. We recycled old pavement, designed new pavers that allow the water to flow into plantings, used native and salt-tolerant plantings, and designed the landscape to slow the water down. But like many pilot projects, the intention of the project preceded changes in the government agencies with jurisdiction over the site, so that many of the green measures either fell by the wayside or became watered down.

In the medians where we did not want people to walk, to direct them away from crossings that are dangerous or confusing, we reused the concrete removed from the old roadbeds and sidewalks, placing them on end and interplanting with yuccas. The result is a kind of hybrid infrastructure garden. Planting alone would not have stood up to the scale of the elevated. The scale of the concrete pieces looked large at first; some critics likened their appearance to tombstones. But as the plants have grown, the scale of the concrete pieces has diminished, and the appearance of the whole has softened.

Concrete from the demolished roadbeds and sidewalks was reused to create this infrastructure landscape.

The final result is a radical departure from a traditional streetscape, in the way it feels as much as in the way it works. It feels like Long Island City: gritty, human-scaled, linked with an august industrial past that included some of the city's premier craftsmen's workshops. But it also feels like a park, a place where people can gather, feel comfortable, find respite. Queens Plaza reinvented is still a tough and industrial landscape, but it is also lush and green.

The resulting landscape integrates movement, planting, water flow, and infrastructure. It doesn't look exactly like the original diagram, but the themes carried through.

The original acoustic analyses suggested that we would not be able to reduce the noise levels from the elevated significantly. Although earth would be the most efficient sound buffer, we could not raise the grade high enough to dampen the sound of the screech. Precedent studies indicated that planting would reduce the noise levels only if they could be wide; a 100-foot-wide swath of trees was considered to be a sufficient buffer, and we only had slivers of space for tree plantings. But a postoccupancy study conducted by the

Landscape Foundation found that the average ambient noise within the open space was reduced by 23 percent. By removing two lanes of traffic that formerly bisected the space and adding lush vegetation, we decreased noise from traffic and the elevated rail lines from a typical range of 85–101 dB to 69–75 dB. That is equivalent to changing the site from the decibel level of Times Square to the level of a Soho street. The man sitting in the photograph at left looks as if he is not terribly disturbed by the traffic coursing through the site (a taxi is visible approximately 20 feet behind him) or the train screeching above.

Bicyclists now have a safer, greener, quieter ride.

Rethinking Boundaries

The issues of who owns what, and off-site issues such as noise, have a huge impact on the way a site can work as a landscape. The way in which a site has been defined should be kept in mind when any project starts. Sometimes reinvention means not only reinvention of the site but reinvention of the idea of ownership or reinvention of the brief, of the assignment altogether. Just because a client tells you that your job is to make a garden, if you understand that no one is going to be able to get to the garden because the entry drive has not been designed to direct you there, you have to say that the garden will work only if you can redesign the entire system of drives. This happens more often than you would think. It's like going to a doctor for a broken finger and finding out that your bones are brittle because of lack of calcium in your diet. You went thinking you would get a splint; instead, you have to change the way you eat and exercise. The same goes for projects: The client may come to you because the plants around the house keep dying, and they want you to choose new ones. You may have to tell this client that you have to regrade the whole property to divert from around the house the water that is drowning the plants and compromising the house's waterproofing. Once you have done that, then you can help with the plantings. But instead of thinking of the plants just around the house, you need to think of the plants over the whole site, because the topography has been changed.

As designers we often accept the contract limit lines that clients and others give us. But once we understand how people circulate through a space—not just within it but as part of a system—or once we understand that there are landscapes or programs that exist outside the project limit line that are critical to the success of the project, it can be necessary to redefine those boundaries. At Queens Plaza, if you didn't look at the surrounding neighborhoods as part of the project, you would have an island rather than a gathering in the fabric. The connections to the citywide bicycle routes, the renovation of Jackson Avenue nearby, the temporary facilities that Outward Bound and community groups were using—these are as much part of the project as the formal limit of the contract. At Queens Plaza, the team was in fact (as is the case in most projects) enjoined from making any changes to any landscape or structure outside the limits of the contract. Sometimes, however, depending on the client and the relationship between a new proposal and adjoining lands, it is possible to say to the client or the community that the limits of the project must be reconsidered in order to make the best landscape for everyone involved. This has been the case on private or institutional projects, where an individual client can possibly acquire more property to make a bigger site. On public projects this is a more difficult exercise, but sometimes it can be proposed.

Proposed Olympic Skating Park, Gangneung, South Korea

At a landfill site in Gangneung, a South Korean seaside city that was proposed as a venue for the 2014 winter Olympics skating arenas, the program could easily fit on the 10 acres provided by the city for the venue. But once

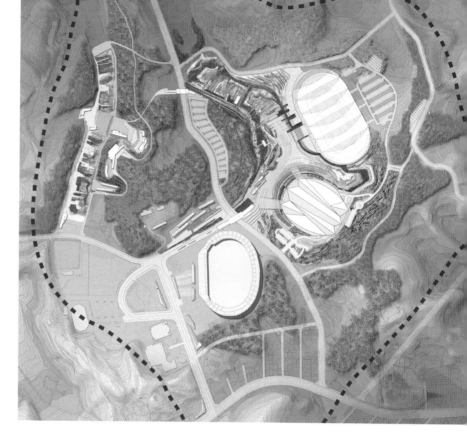

Revised project boundary, to include surrounding farm fields and create a park loop.

the Olympics were over, the new landscape would remain as a cul-de-sac, a recreational dead end at the top of a hill. By looking beyond the boundary of the project to a network of rice fields that connect to the urban landscape below, the planners and designers could amass enough land for a 28-acre park network. This new network would take in the landfill plus a corridor of agricultural land and provide connections to the rest of the city. After the Olympics, the open space would play a role in the health of the city.

The open space on the landfill site could be designed to remediate the unfortunate toxic conditions of the site, which had been improperly capped, and connect with a larger open space network linked to the city's existing parks. If the planners and designers were to accept the limited boundaries of the project, the terraced landscape below, which showcases the filtration of polluted water from underneath the cap, would have been shoehorned into a dead end of the site. But as part of a new open space network, it is the gateway into the more formalized landscape at the arenas and a major park circulation space.

After the Olympics, the venue becomes a winter park.

The contaminated water from below grade on the landfill flows through the extensive constructed wetlands, leading to the more plaza-like spaces. The harder paved urban landscape is a place for people for all seasons, for the life of the Olympics but also for the life of the city.

Finally, reinvention is about changing the way a place works, looks, and feels; it most often will completely change the way people perceive a place and use it. We have thankfully reached the end of the era when photographs of landscapes in books and magazines never have any people in them. Our work, more often than not, is about how people use spaces, how they live in places, what they do, how they walk, dance, play, and rest. Designing for people has the added benefit of empowering a proprietary population, people who will not only care about but care for the landscape.

Not so long ago, functions such as remediation of pollution or even how people used space were factors that a designer might feel impelled to include in a design, overlaid onto a formal plan. Or not. As designers of active urban places we see the energy of these uses as generating the life of the landscape, producing the rhythms that become landscape design. And in reinventing a site such as a hard urban infrastructure or a toxic landfill, unless we reinvent the way people use the site we will not have made a place that really works.

The filtration garden cleans the poorly treated water from the landfill.

Chapter 3:

Restoration

The idea of restoration could seem, on the surface, antithetical to design. In the decades since the environmental movement took hold, any self-respecting high-design practice couldn't help but marginalize the concept of restoration. Restoration was what people with no imaginations did. Design made something new; restoration just put back what was there. Interviewing landscape designers and contractors for a residential project in Santa Fe sometime around 1995, I mentioned that I wanted to use pinyon and juniper—the plants that dominate the high desert woodland of the region— outside the house. One English garden–inclined landscape designer, when asked whether she could do this, could not have looked less enthusiastic. "Yes, I could do that," she told me grudgingly. "It really is just a *restoration* project, but I can find the plants for you."

However, restoration is not a textbook scientific method, nor is it in any way dull. The research, planning, and design involved can engage an intensely creative process. In order to restore a landscape, you have to know what it has been over time, what it has become, and where it probably is going. Just deciding exactly what needs to be restored calls for decisions that are not necessarily scientific. The act of restoration can range from trying to make things look exactly as they were at a specific point in time to making a landscape that restores certain environmental processes but looks nothing like the original. On landscape projects we most commonly conceive of restoration as the process of bringing a disturbed site back in line with what it was before. Yet the time frame can range from a matter of years to millennia. We can restore slopes that have been eroded by recent construction, slowing water down and revegetating. Or we can restore wetlands that disappeared hundreds of years ago, before Europeans landed on American shores, for instance, and began filling in wetlands to create more buildable land. The act of restoration can range from remediating local conditions caused by a current project to reestablishing long-lost habitat.

Restoration can also entail restoring connections, restoring scale, restoring functions. It can mean restoring long-lost practices. In order to do the work of restoration, it is essential to do enough homework, and make enough connections with people who know a place, to understand what might be restored. You may be asked to restore a particular bridge over a creek. But unless you restore some of the upstream permeable surfaces—undertaking an ecological restoration when the formal restoration task in the brief is cultural—and the banks of the creeks, the bridge may very well be washed away when the creek floods, due to unchecked water volumes.

The site for the Living Water Park was selected sheerly on size, in order to filter as much polluted water as possible. The largest site available happened to be at a spot on the Fu River across from an amusement park with a ferris wheel.

In 1996 I went to work on the Living Water Park in Chengdu, Sichuan, China, with artist Betsy Damon. Our first orders of business were to select a site for the new park, which would demonstrate how water can be cleansed biologically, and to interview all the players, from horticulturists to recreation managers. When asked what they wanted the park to do, many of the local landscape architects and technical consultants said they wanted a three-part narrative, and they all outlined the following story line: "This is what nature used to be, this is how humans have damaged nature, and this is how we can make it better." I was impressed by how many people conceived of this narrative as critical to the project. And indeed this narrative can be seen at the Living Water Park: You see the murky river water in the static settling pond, then you can walk down along the flow forms that spin the water around, aerating it and, according to biodynamic theory, restoring it to a healthy molecular structure. You can walk through the constructed wetlands and learn how the plants pull pollutants out of the water; and then you find the still pools of filtered water at the end of the process, clean enough for people to wade in.

This restoration narrative does not actually prove that we can restore the landscape to what it was before human presence. And that isn't necessarily the goal. We can't, just from records or memory, know exactly what the landscape was before, nor can we know that the landscape will somehow be able to exist, in the future, as it once was. The Living Water Park does not attempt to reverse the process of degradation, but this narrative is ambitious, attempting to restore water biologically to a clean state and to restore the landscape to a healthy state that is self-sustaining.

A less ambitious program for restoration simply aims to reverse certain negative impacts on the landscape, such as erosion, deforestation, or the proliferation of invasive species. Erosion can be addressed via sustainable stormwater management, revegetation, or a combination of the two. Deforestation can be reversed by appropriate plant species selection and planting culture. Combating invasive species is less clear cut: The attitude that exotic or invasive species are necessarily bad has come under scrutiny in recent years, particularly by authors Rick Darke and Doug Tallamy, whose work promotes the use of native plants within a strictly functional framework. They argue that plants formerly called "exotic invasives" may not prevent the local ecosystem from functioning. If the food web is functioning so that most species can be sustained, then a plant that is exotic may not be so bad. Their work questions the idea of eliminating species that did not formerly exist on a site and focuses rather on moving ahead into a future where these hard-line classifications may no longer make sense. We can attempt to restore a hardwood landscape in a northern climate, but the temperatures have shifted, and the landscape sustains many climatic disruptions that did not previously exist. We are in an age when purism may not be an appropriate response. Ironically, the less cut-and-dried approach may call for a greater understanding of how a particular ecosystem is working. Even the less ambitious practice of "spot" restoration depends on a whole system understanding of ecological functioning.

We talk of restoration landscapes as having been disturbed. Our concept of disturbance can often ignore the interaction of human processes with those of plants, animals, water, and all other realms we consider "natural." The classic story of the American landscape told by William Cronon in his landmark book *Changes in the Land* belies the myth that the landscape before European settlement was untouched; he chronicles the symbiotic relationship between Native Americans and the forests of the Northeast, which involved intense human management of the environment, including controlled burns. Once you dig deeper into the governing concepts in the process of restoration, you find only more ambiguity and complexity. What *disturbance*, *invasive*, *exotic*, and of course *natural* really mean becomes less and less clear.

Any project for which the scope includes "restoration" has to go through a process of study, for the planners and designers to understand exactly what restoration means for this site, this client, and this program. We have all sorts of ideas about what restoration is, and it is important to understand the many nuances of the term. Many words float around the term *restoration*, such as *reclamation* and *remediation*, and it's helpful to understand the distinctions between them.

Refraining from Thinking One Word Means One Thing

On projects where the goal is habitat restoration, there are a number of operations that can happen sequentially or be phased for some to happen at the same time. If you simply restore a plant community but do not deal with animals that can forage or trample new plantings, your project will fail. So first you need to think of what you need to *exclude*, large mammals being the easiest, reptiles probably being among the most difficult. Same goes for invasive species: If you want to reestablish a plant community but don't plan for how an exotic plant might try to outcompete the new plantings, your project will fail. So you need to figure out what plants or species you need to *eradicate*.

Then you have to look at the condition of the site. Are there patches of bare earth that will erode and compromise the restoration? You have to figure out whether you need to *stabilize* the existing landscape to prevent something like erosion or flooding from happening.

Although sometimes subtle, there is a difference between stabilizing and *reclaiming*. We can stabilize areas that are degraded but that we would like to continue functioning as they have, such as the eroded slopes at Shillim, a 2,500-acre retreat in India. But transforming a part of the site so that it will function differently programmatically or ecologically—demolishing a road, for instance, and revegetating the excavated swath to attract wildlife— is reclamation. In mining, the concept carries with it an idea of what the land will be used for once it has been restored; it is the engineering of derelict terrain so that it can be used for some purpose. What parts of the site would you like to erase and turn into something that fits into your larger program, environmental or otherwise? Utility areas, roads, drives, paths, and building footprints disappear and reemerge as part of a larger ecological system.

On many reclamation projects, we are not simply taking a piece of land back or making it wild again; rather, we are *remediating* some unhealthful conditions such as contaminants in the soils. The Living Water Park demonstrates how plants can remediate water pollution; in instances where the contaminants cannot be metabolized by plants, as in the case of chromium, the site can be remediated only by removing the soil to a certain depth, often capped, and covering it with new soils.

Remediation projects tackle major degradation. On projects where there is not a huge amount that is not working—a forest that is functioning fine, regenerating and largely free of invasives, but could be more diverse, for instance—we sometimes work just to improve the forest, simply *enhancing* what is there.

But you might ask whether enhancing a site is not reinventing it as habitat or as a place to live. This is where the overlap between strategies is clear. They are not exclusive; one component in the reinvention of a site may be the restoration of certain systems. At Queens Plaza, the connection between the north and south sides of the Queensboro Bridge and elevated trains has been restored. It is not merely a matter of semantics but of emphasis. At Queens Plaza, our task was to reinvent the place, to propel it into a state no one had experienced before. On a project you may classify as a restoration project, the emphasis is on return.

For a project in the tropics, the client, an environmental organization that bought a camplike school that had been abandoned, wanted to restore the native forest, which had been disturbed over many years when students and teachers trampled the earth on a daily basis. When we began reviewing what needed to be done in order to "restore," there were several different communities to restore but also many different processes. The disturbances fell into four categories: foraging by exotic mammals such as deer, trampling by humans, proliferation of invasive species, and erosion caused by altered drainage ways or deforestation The first was to exclude the foraging exotic mammals by fencing the site. Quite often we discourage fencing, because it can exclude native mammals and cut off wildlife corridors. But in this area of the tropics there were no native terrestrial animals, so exclusion would keep out the exotics that did most of the damage but not cut off any lifelines for wildlife. This was not the approach at Shillim, where grazing and slash-and-burn agriculture had stripped the lower slopes of vegetation, resulting in large-scale erosion. Because the 2,500-acre site is a corridor for many fauna including endangered members of the cat family, the decision was made not to fence. Instead, the exclusion consisted of stationing guards around the perimeter to prevent people from coming onto the site to graze or cut down trees.

The environmental institute project was sited on a much more disturbed site. We looked at what invasive exotics to eradicate, to determine whether there was a need to remove certain species that were choking out others. One challenge for restoration in this climate, where a long dry season is followed by torrential rains, and on this topography that sloped toward the sea, is the staging of eradication. The area of removals has to be replanted and take root almost immediately, or the bare earth will erode; new plantings have to be done at the right time to get the benefit of the rainy season without being so young that they will get washed away. The teachers and students had planted patches of exotic plants over the years, including crotons and snake plant. Walking around with the ecologists, we noted many patches of snake plant, but because snake plant grows clonally, by sending new shoots underground via the roots, and the clonal patches do not enlarge very quickly, the plant did not seem to be a short-term threat. Generally the snake plant grew in areas of secondary importance, along paths. However, the croton had been planted around all the buildings, and now that the buildings were gone the idea was to restore native habitat on the old footprints. The croton would choke out any native plantings we would do there, so that was one (fairly easy to remove) plant that could use some eradication. So rather than launching a costly all-out eradication campaign, we opted to prioritize, proposing to eradicate the croton first and leave the snake plant because it was not interfering with other plants or features in the short term and because we had many other concerns to address immediately.

Several adverse conditions other than invasive species compromised not only the terrestrial landscape but marine life as well. Bare earth left by the removal of the school buildings would pose erosion problems; the existing paved areas sped up large volumes of water that washed loose soils downhill and into the water. The sediment levels in the water measured many times higher than was normal, and the harm to corals and other sea life was visible. So we had to assign a high priority to simply stabilizing the earth. We didn't know long term what the best course of action was to be, so we had to come up with a short-term strategy. Sometimes in the planning process you can hold off on acting—whether it is restoration or another strategy—because you do not have enough information, consensus, or money for the whole initiative. But if you delay because you want to get the whole process just right, many organisms, from plankton to coral to fish, can die while you are crafting the perfect restoration plan. So we had to plan for a short-term stabilization plan to tide us over until a comprehensive environmental management plan could be completed. We could regrade the worst drainage ways and plant with a cover crop, leaving open the possibility of a different mode of revegetation in the future. So we came up with a preliminary site work plan, which we planned to implement while we were in preliminary design phases.

Quite often you run parallel tracks on a project, in concept on one aspect but zooming in to schematic on others; in this case, we would begin the process of short-term restoration of the most disturbed and vulnerable areas of erosion while we had not completed a comprehensive concept plan for the program. Running parallel phases is something we all do but rarely formalize. If you formalize these phases and understand that there may be multiple phases at once, you can act quickly to avoid further damage to the landscape.

The key to running parallel tracks efficiently and successfully is to enumerate every single operation that will need to be done and develop an environmental management plan—saying what is going to happen, where, and when—on a timeline. Getting the team together to plan for how the work will be implemented will tease out any conflicts or overlaps; conflicts can be avoided through better scheduling, and overlaps can be capitalized, as there are economies of scale in doing a number of operations at once.

The bluffs overlooking the Atlantic Ocean at the end of Long Island represent a unique geological formation that distinguishes Montauk, the island's land's end, from the wide, sandy beaches of the Hamptons. For generations, people built houses on these bluffs. The bluffs support unique plant and animal life; this portion of bluff had been scalped, literally stripped, during construction for a pool that was eventually resited more reasonably inboard of the house. The bluff was regraded and planted with native grasses that grow naturally on these slopes, stabilizing them and creating cover for birds and other creatures. The primary program, however, was access to the beach. This bluff was not only restored, it was reclaimed as a way of moving through a wild landscape and down to the beach.

In the Caribbean school site there were several *Eugenia* species that occurred in low quantities on the lower slopes of the site, where there was more disturbance; one component of the "restoration" of the forest might be just to interplant more of a species that is in low numbers, improving wildlife habitat.

Finally, there are times when you will be completely *recreating* the profile of a particular biome. In the Caribbean project, we proposed to reclaim the roads to manage stormwater better, regrading to create bioswales that would slow the water down and allow the water to percolate into the groundwater, reducing the amount of stormwater and sediment that reached the sea. But we proposed a minimal list of species because we wanted to optimize the area's function as a kind of sponge and so would stick to the sturdiest species. The result would not resemble anything that grew on the site previously; the ribbons of former road reclaimed could take on a sculptural quality. On another area, however, where several utility buildings on a leveled area of land were being demolished, we could recreate the natural grade and then attempt to recreate the dry forest that surrounded the cleared area.

Particularly on urban projects, we often encounter sites where water has become polluted by sewage, manufacturing waste, nutrients from chemical fertilizers, or pesticides from agricultural and domestic uses. Soils have become contaminated by heavy metals, herbicides, and pesticides. Remediation is the first order of business, before we consider whether programming for people to be able to use the space is even feasible.

An eroded slope can be remediated by revegetating with a cover that will hold the soil. When dealing with contaminated water or soils we use phytoremediation, using plants to cleanse the material. Particular contaminants can be successfully metabolized, and thereby removed from the soil or water, by plants, remediating pollution. The Living Water Park, a 6-acre park in Chengdu, Sichuan, China, is a demonstration of phytoremediation and a symbol of the restoration of natural processes to the city.

Bringing Natural Processes Back into the City

The Living Water Park, Chengdu, Sichuan, China

The Living Water Park was designed as a demonstration of how water can be cleansed biologically, through a sequence of settlement, filtration, and aeration.

Constructed wetlands, with the city beyond.

The lessons from the Living Water Park have lasted me many years, influencing the way I work in teams and also the way I think formally, in terms of design form. I often operate with a much more layered approach, layering different activities and ecological ideas with formal moves and gestures.

All of our work—landscape, architecture, planning—can help remediate environmental problems such as pollution, poor soils, and flooding. The Living Water Park shows how different plants can metabolize contaminants in the Fu River's water, including heavy metals. One of the first contemporary demonstrations of phytoremediation as landscape form was conceptual artist Mel Chin's "Revival Field," a project he began in 1990 with Dr. Rufus Chaney, a senior agronomist from the US Department of Agriculture (USDA). Chin planted ninety-six test situations of six different plant species in circular 'plots' and then delivered samples to Dr. Chaney's USDA lab. The results of this artwork, which measured the amount of heavy metal uptake by the different species, confirmed the scientific technology of phytoremediation by special plants called hyperaccumulators.

DEMONSTRATING NATURAL PROCESSES

At the Living Water Park, the polluted water from the Fu River is pumped up into a pump house that doubles as a teahouse; then out into a settlement pond, where the solids and particulates settle to the floor of the pond, to be cleaned out every other year or so; then through a series of flow forms, which aerate the water; then into a series of constructed wetlands.

Proponents of Rudolf Steiner's biodynamics theories believe that flow forms actually change the molecular structure of the water, returning it to a pure state. While preparing for my trip to Chengdu, I called up several hydrologists, including my hydrology professor from Harvard, to ask them

The water is pumped up into a settlement pond, where the solids settle to the bottom, to be cleaned out periodically.

Flow forms designed by environmental artist Betsy Damon.

whether there is any way that the molecular structure of water could change, just by spinning around in a spiral form, from polluted to healthy. No way, they all said, in various degrees of either shock or amusement at my latest venture. After pondering their answers, and the answers of those who disagree with them in the many articles on flow forms, I decided that I didn't care. The sculptures are lovely to look at, the water is definitely healthier, from the oxygenation caused by all that spinning around, and it just feels great to be near them. Although I worked with scientists, my final criterion on a project such as the Living Water Park is whether we have made a place that not only functions better but also looks and feels better. If the flow forms operate only to aerate the water, and the claims for changing the molecular structure of water have no grounds, it doesn't matter to me. If it does not work as a place where people, or wildlife, want to be then it certainly does matter.

When environmental artist Betsy Damon invited me to work on the Living Water Park, she had been organizing art installations on the city's rivers over the previous 8 or so years. Large-scale environmental works by her and by Chinese artists she mobilized spoke to the degradation

The water filtration landscape was designed for people as well as natural processes.

of the water but also pointed toward a kind of redemption through restoring natural processes that would cleanse the polluted river water. One of Betsy's works was a performance called "Washing Silk." The piece consisted of a group of women washing white silk in the river, harking back to one of the many daily rituals that connected people with the rivers before they became dumping grounds. But instead of washing the white silk with their bare hands, as they would have traditionally, the women wore bright orange hazmat-like gloves; the silk, as they washed, became less and less white, taking on the murky gray of the polluted river water. Many of Chengdu's environmental stewards—including the head of the FuNan Rivers Renovation Bureau—took notice of these installations and performances. Eventually they asked Betsy to put together a proposal for creating a park dedicated to cleaning up polluted river water.

When I visited Chengdu in 1996 it was still a bicycle city, with schools of bicyclists claiming the center of the roads and the odd cars on the sides; the main city hospital had been built in the 1940s and had retractable doors like an airplane hangar so that in the summer it was almost open air. But the city was undergoing a huge change: Much of the old city was being torn down and highrises built. The economy was booming, and more people were able to afford cars. Just 3 years later, in 1999, when I returned to see the completed project, the ratio of cars to bicycles had flipped, with the cars driving in schools and the bicyclists as the oddities at the roadsides. The idea of a city as a place where natural processes occur was largely disappearing. When I arrived in Chengdu I didn't quite know what my job was supposed to be; Betsy had told me only that we were going to design a park that would clean polluted river water. The park was intended to teach people about phytoremediation, the biological cleansing of earth and water by plants; in this case it was the water in need of cleansing. The first morning after I arrived, I walked with Betsy

Betsy Damon first drew attention to the water quality of Chengdu's rivers with performance pieces such as "Washing Silk." This piece highlighted the ill health of the river, and the passing of the tradition of washing in the river, as the color of the silk turned from pure white to dirty gray; the women wore orange hazmat gloves.

Damon and her physicist son, John Otto, into a conference meeting at the FuNan Rivers Renovation Bureau office. This was the official kickoff meeting, with representatives from the environmental agencies, parks, recreation, sanitation, housing, the universities, all seated around the longest conference table I had ever seen. A serial array of centerpieces with a crossed pair of flags ran down the center.

At this meeting, the form of communication was serial declamation. After the mayor's deputy called the meeting to order, each representative stood, one at a time, around the table, delivering a speech that (thanks to Mr. Li Jian, my translator and collaborator) I understood to begin with the same message: "We are very grateful to the city and to the mayor, or the head of the FuNan Rivers Renovation Bureau, for providing this opportunity for us to create for Chengdu a truly modern park that will be a beacon to other cities in China. This project builds on the work we have already done in establishing Chengdu as a model of landscape for the country; these are our hopes for the park." And then each would outline the wishes of his or her (and there were plenty of women representatives around the table) agency, which ranged from providing for the highest-quality recreation space to supporting the city's effort to clean up its waterways via the construction of the city's first sewage treatment plant. Afterwards, however, I reflected on this unusual meeting and thought, "What if we conducted meetings like this in the United States? How many time hogs around the conference table would we deter, as each person gets a turn to talk? How many people who have great ideas or programs but lack nerve would be able to contribute?" The meeting was also a godsend for me, as I got to sit and take everything in and not have to say anything of any intelligence.

I still didn't know exactly what my scope of work was, nor what Betsy intended to do herself. I looked around at the meeting, and at the subsequent afternoon sessions with each agency head. It was just me, Betsy, and John, listening and taking notes. There were many players on this team and no one person saying who was going to do what, when, and how. I eventually facilitated a group of architects, landscape architects, scientists, engineers, and artists, among others, to draw up a schematic design that achieved the goals of the project: to create a destination park that could work both as refuge for the city and as a demonstration of how we can remediate environmental ills. When we interviewed many of the team members, particularly the city's landscape architects, about what they wanted for the Living Water Park, each outlined the same vision for the park's narrative. They all wanted to tell the three-part story: This is the way our natural world was, before we built up our cities, this is how our development led to pollution of the environment, and this is how we can clean it up.

We had the brief, we had the team; the only thing missing was a site. This is not a unique experience in practice. I have worked on a number of projects that had a clear mission and a salaried staff—but no site. My job with Patric O'Malley of Gensler to help start up the Hudson Rivers and Estuaries Center consisted of visiting something like twenty-five sites on the Hudson River, studying the feasibility or appropriateness of each for the center, and narrowing the alternative sites down to three, and then to one. Our job is sometimes to say not only what a place should be but where. In the case of the Rivers and Estuaries Center, a site in Beacon, New York was selected for the following reasons: It sat in one of those iconic Hudson River landscapes, with the highlands, Bear Mountain, and Garrison to the south; it had abandoned historic and industrial buildings on the site, which could be reused; and it linked to an existing state park. And finally, unlike some of the most dramatic sites, such as the old Alcoa plant in Hastings, which literally sits out in the river facing the Palisades, the site was big enough.

In Chengdu, we had a list of eight potential sites along the 90 miles of riverfront. The team set out on a 3-day tour of all the potential sites—some of them beautiful, many industrial, one at the confluence of the Fu and Nan rivers, a cultural crossroads that boasted a teahouse and many monuments. After several days of reviewing the sites, we returned to the office, and Betsy asked me my opinion, I think imagining that I would give her a nuanced analysis of the pros and cons of many sites. But the answer was easy in this case. In order to filter polluted water, you need a large amount of space, about 1 cubic foot of constructed wetland for every gallon of water. Plant species sitting with their roots inundated with water pull the heavy metals and other contaminants up through their roots and out of the water. The more acreage we had, the more significant a demonstration this would be. So the site selection process seemed inanely obvious to me: We just needed to select the largest site, to allow for enough filtration to demonstrate the cleansing process. A raw open space—made raw by the demolition of housing along the river, to create 90 miles of riverfront park—at the northeastern corner of the axial city came to 6 acres, the largest area of any of the eight or so available sites. I was glad that we toured all the sites because it gave me an opportunity to take the place in. I came from a design culture where large minimal gestures had become almost a given in landscape design. Parks with a more domestic scale within them were considered fussy or Disney-like. I was used to large patterns, layouts of one system over a whole site. Chengdu's park spaces were more like nested landscapes. I saw park after park where small-scale space— a vignette of a bridge over water leading to a pavilion set in a hillside of rocks and trees, a "poet's house" commemorating Li Bao—sat within a

The plan for the Rivers and Estuaries Center in Beacon, New York called for extensive constructed wetlands surrounding the decommissioned paper clip factory.

larger park, like a private residential compound. The places for people to come together were compressed spaces, or so they seemed to me, given my Western design training. This sense of intensely packed spaces would help with the programming of the Living Water Park for multiple uses, cultural and recreational as well as interpretive. So the park would showcase river restoration, but it would also provide intimate places for people to gather, meet, put their feet in the water, and find relief from the baking hot summer weather. This integration of a complex series of scales within one project was also to have an indelible impact on the way I approach the issue of scale on most planning and design projects.

One of the lessons I learned in Chengdu in 1996 was to check my preconceptions and my emotionally based biases at the door. That year in Chengdu, more than 100,000 people were being relocated from old, traditional courtyard housing at the river's edge to new, modern housing blocks. I took many photographs of the beautiful tile-roofed traditional houses, rapidly collapsing under the bulldozers.

The city was in a state of wholesale demolition: 90 miles of riverfront were being rebuilt, and new conduit for the city's first centralized water treatment system was laid just behind the new river walls; old, low buildings were coming down as new highrises went up. A gray haze of construction dust hung in the air, powdering the cypresses, cedars, and other evergreens that gave Chengdu the reputation as a great Garden City of China. Neighborhoods lay in rubble as huge conduit was laid behind a new river wall, constructed outboard of the ancient wall that sometimes stepped down to the water, sometimes sloped evenly, sometimes jogged around the ghost of a demolished house or temple.

Ninety miles of riverfront were rebuilt as Chengdu modernized rapidly in the late 1990s. New sewer lines were built behind the new flood walls, taking wastewater to the city's first wastewater treatment plant.

The rebuilt riverfront provided a uniform, and somewhat sterile, treatment to the water's edge.

After the first few days of feeling desolate about the history of this city and these dwellings, including a number of Taoist temples, disappearing within the space of a couple of months, I started to talk with my teammates, through my fellow landscape architect and translator, Mr. Li Jian, about this "renovation" project. The houses, with no heat, hot water, or insulation, were so basic, most inhabitants were happy to gain the modern amenities offered by the new highrises. The old houses were referred to as hovels, and when we discussed whether they could be retrofitted with modern conveniences, I understood that it is only in an affluent society such as ours was at the time that anyone would have the means to modernize a seventeenth-century house, for instance. For the hundreds of thousands of Chendgu residents who had lived for generations with substandard conditions, the move to modern blocks was, in terms of utilities and comfort, a move forward and upward. The social life—multigenerational families, neighbors sharing open space—that courtyard housing engenders may have been lost in the move to double-loaded corridors, but at least the residents would be warm, with hot water for washing.

The Living Water Park was to be the crown jewel in this tremendous campaign to remediate poor living conditions in the city, most notably the lack of a water treatment system. The process of cleansing water biologically became something of a metaphor for how Chengdu was reinventing itself as a modern, clean city.

The cleansing part needed to be demonstrable and proven. The team's microbiologist took the lead on this, handing us the diagram on page 96 to specify the depths of water that would support the plants and organisms that can cleanse the water. So while we organized the park around the three-part narrative—showing in stark contrast the murky water as it is pumped up from the river, then as it flows into constructed wetlands, as it flows over aeration surfaces and in flow form sculptures, and then out into a wading pool—we also organized the park according to the depth diagram. We used the diagram to determine how high we needed to bring up the grade of the pump house so that the system could work through gravity, allowing for the slow movement of the water downhill through the root zones of the plants.

Many of the plants on the diagram show up consistently on the universally recognized list of invasive species: phragmites, cattail, water hyacinth. But in this situation, where they are contained they are valuable plants that, because they are such adapters and survivors, can not only tolerate high levels of pollution but metabolize the pollutants, leaving the water cleaner. Where a balance of species and relative health of the ecosystem remains, invasive species are considered a threat. But where a system has been messed up, and you need to bring in the big guns that can pull contaminants out of water or soil, invasive species are the stars of the show.

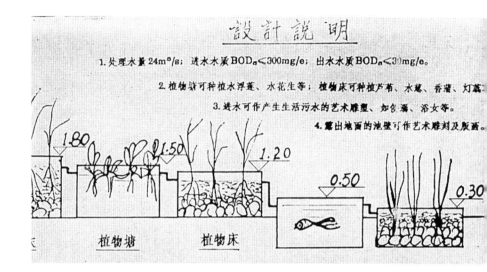

The Living Water Park was the first water-cleansing park in China; in addition, and separately from the cleansing focus, it was also the first park in China to showcase native plants.

LEARNING FROM EACH OTHER

Working on projects internationally raises critical questions about what we are doing and why. Are we joining a team to work collaboratively? Are we sharing information and practices? Are we exporting our expertise? Because of the technical nature of this project, before I arrived a number of scientists had been invited to join the team, and the restoration of the river engaged many different disciplines: ecologists, hydrologists, microbiologists, and archaeologists. Arriving on a project of this scope with so much on-the-ground information and science, the job of the landscape architect is not to make a proposal but to get everyone together and help synthesize. Maybe the distance of the foreigner helps orient the group. After a few days in Chengdu I realized that it was not just river water that was going to be restored; it was also some traditional practices that had fallen out of favor.

Plants that can cleanse water are often invasive in uncontained spaces. The water hyacinths, here contained in narrow beds, can overtake a waterbody if unchecked.

Oxygenating plants absorb excess nutrients in the water and release oxygen, deterring the growth of unwanted algae.

Cattails are considered invasive in some environments; they make up the majority of the biomass at the Living Water Park.

I arrived in Chengdu to a riverfront that was being reclaimed for public use, with the 90 linear miles of riverfront on the Fu and Nan Rivers formerly occupied by housing and occasional other uses, rebuilt as waterfront park. When city officials showed us the designs for much of the 90 miles, it was apparent that the waterfront was being redesigned according to modern

standards, with concrete paving units and large swaths of plantings. And in fact the style—abstract patterns, beautifully done, but almost graphic on the ground—seemed to me to have been imported from the States. It looked like a lot of public parks that had come, in the United States, to seem conventional.

I gradually gleaned that one of my jobs on this project was to redirect the focus onto the existing local parks, where paving had been done for eons using river stone and mortar. Although I know I was there because of the belief by some members of the local team that international designers could "elevate" the project, there were many others who were relieved to be able to design the Living Water Park according to practices they had been following for generations, but using them as an authentic art form and not out of

Traditional method of paving with river stone.

Traditional river stone integrated with concrete flow forms.

nostalgia. I left feeling that I was involved more in a cultural exchange than in an international drive-by landscaping solution. Cultural exchange can do as much to clarify one's own identity as it can broaden one's experience of others. The process of restoration enabled age-old traditions of craftsmanship to flourish in a way that I am not sure the team would have felt comfortable pushing for in light of the prevailing taste for contemporary design. My presence there reflected back to the team who they were and what they knew how to do, what they wanted to do new but also what they wanted to do as their predecessors had done for a long time.

Every project, every site, every client is different. Every process of restoration will be different; for instance, the use of phragmites may be deployed to remediate pollution across the world, but the practices and

Larger river stones used to retain water edges.

culture of design will be different. Many designers make money through repetition. By rolling out designs that have been done before—an actual layout, or a style—architecture and landscape firms can capitalize on their expertise. But if you take each project as a new matrix of site, design team, and client, it is almost impossible to do the same design twice. For the Living Water Park, not only could I not promote a preplanned method of design, but I had to check many of my most viscerally held methods at the gate. My formal training came into question in a stark and instructive way. For this restoration project, the language of design needed to be safeguarded. The story of restoration could be told not abstractly but through a common language of metaphor and association. The scientific facts could amaze, but the use of familiar symbols would resonate.

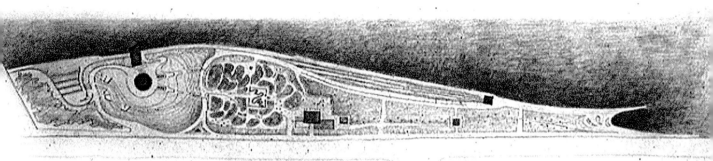

When I started to plan out the flow of water through the landscape on the site, the aerial plan started to take on the shape of a fish, because of the bow shape of the plot of land; because of the settlement pond, which looked like an eye; and because of the constructed wetlands, designed using local methods for terracing farmland, which came to resemble either internal organs or scales. This fish-ness had me very worried; after all, I had passed through 3 years of graduate school at Harvard, where the term *literal* was the kiss of death. Abstraction was the norm; anything representational or figurative—anything that was recognizable as something other than a landscape—was considered unsophisticated. This training led me to feel strikingly out of my comfort zone in the presence of literal representation. So the second week, after I had laid out all the ideas the team had developed—the narrative, the gravity flow, the circulation—I tried to make the plan look less like a fish, angling the lines and blurring the scales. When the local landscape architects came to work on it, they took one look at the first draft plan pinned up on the wall and said, with a lot of enthusiasm, "Great! It looks like a fish." They were encouraged because the fish is a sign of good health and good fortune. The fish-ness was an asset, both for them internally in their own design processes and for the whole team in explaining the project to others. I stood back and looked; "Okay," I thought, "I need to embrace the fish." It might actually turn out to be a handsome fish, but it definitely needed some work if we were going to go that route. So after our working session I went over to the market across the street from our little hotel, paid a visit to the fishmonger, and spent a long time drawing the fish as they wriggled in plastic buckets. I tried to make the plan look even more like a fish, drawing out the river terraces almost like a mouth and gills, and I must admit that the act of creating a plan so literal felt magnificently liberating. It felt really good to drop my habits and join in with another group's mindset. The process drove home for me the lesson that we can't arrive on the scene with a solution. We have to feel our way, through the site, and through the team process. At the Living Water Park the restoration did not stop at polluted water; the process tapped into the zeitgeist of the time in Chengdu and restored some of the practices that had been suppressed for a few decades.

The ratings systems and checklists tell you what to do or not to do, but rarely do they tell you how to do it. The design process should be your first subject of design. Your average checklist, whether it's from Leadership in Energy and Environmental Design or from a professional practice course, may not tell you how to develop a multidisciplinary team that includes local and international players and how to ensure that the local designers take on significant and meaningful roles in the design process. The Living Water Park process worked partly because my engagement on the project was limited. I traveled there for a limited amount of time, a little under a month, and then I left. Had I remained on the team, I would have probably discouraged a lot of the breakdown of scale, addition of programs, and general creation of more "stuff." Words such as *overdesign*, *clutter*, *busy*—words like this have traditionally been considered a smackdown in the Western modernist idiom in which I was trained. Luckily for the project, I left once my work was done, and the project took on a life of its own.

The design became more complex once the local team started to work on it.

Betsy Damon remained, to develop the design of the individual flow forms, and to shepherd the project through construction, while local professionals took on major roles in developing the landscape and architecture. The drawing I left with Betsy and the local team was a skeletal framework, which

over the next year they put life into. The artists and designers who took the design through construction layered and layered it, and in fact now it is in keeping with the more traditional riverfront parks in Chengdu, where the scale of public landscapes can be garden scale, with footbridges, small pagoda-like shelters, and koi ponds, plenty of places to explore and discover. A more minimalist scheme would have worked on many fewer levels.

A local architect developed the series of details, where water is aerated as it is let out of a still pool. My translator was also the lead landscape architect; in getting to know each other so closely because of my need for a translator, we had a very easy rapport when we turned to design.

An amphitheater has become a popular place for games.

Traditional signage and
lighting along a park path.

The scale and density, the intensity, of the spaces is specific to a landscape style common to Chengdu parks.

CONNECTING LOCALLY

In most restoration projects, it is critical to forge the local connections that are going to make the process meaningful and sustainable. Many local practitioners developed the design of the Living Water Park, and its success is due to how responsive the design was to the program and community. A local architect completed the design for the pump house/teahouse, very much in keeping with local traditions of craftsmanship and detailed paving designs. Local horticulturists developed the plantings to include many native plants at the edges of the constructed wetlands.

When I returned to see the completed park in 1999, I was amazed to see how much program they had inserted into the simple park plan: an amphitheater, two concession stands, and an environmental center. In addition, the teahouse, which we had suggested be at the highest level of the pump house, at the level of the settlement pond, rose two more floors above that and was packed with people year-round.

The place in the park where I felt this lesson—that my job was in some ways to reorient and reflect back, and not to rely on certain design habits of mine—most keenly was at the river terraces. Whereas the majority of the park is thronged with people during the warm months, this permeable paving terrace leading down to the water is almost always empty.

When I returned to the States after visiting the completed park, in 1999, some of my architect friends were bewildered by the "lava-like" forms of the constructed wetlands and thought the project was unpublishable; the formal

The pumphouse was conceived as a teahouse, in keeping with the tradition of riverfront teahouses throughout the Fu and Nan Rivers.

The teahouse has become a bustling social center.

language that was more organic than geometric seemed to them to be "anti-design." The only part of the project any of them liked was the minimalist river terrace down to the water. Yet it was this part of the project that was the least popular. Looking at the many fantastic parks in Chengdu, it is unusual to find large, unbroken planes of space, except at formal staging areas and ceremonial paved spaces. Such "emptiness" perhaps seems as uninviting to many people who live in Chengdu as the "lava-like" forms of the Living Water Park were once (very recently) considered "anti-design" by many of my colleagues. Restoration in this case depended on respect for the way people have traditionally conceived of and used space in the parks of Chengdu.

The permeable river terrace—the one part of the design the author's architect colleagues thought elegant—is one of the least popular spots in the park.

A narrower portion of the river terrace

PROVIDING WAYS FOR PEOPLE TO ENJOY THE PROCESS

Western designers may have been shocked by the design of the Living Water Park: the organic forms, the literalness, the lack of any sleek gestures (aside from those unpopular river terraces). But now it has become a model for other parks in China and for students all over the world who write to me and to Betsy.

And it is a place where people are as comfortable posing for wedding photos as they are learning about how water can be cleansed biologically.

Stapleton, Staten Island, New York City

When we are called to look at a project, we are not necessarily given the charge of ecological restoration in the brief. But a broader conception of restoration is often on the agenda. Quite often the main driver of a project does not include restoring "natural" systems. Sometimes what we are asked

All along the route, children enjoy being in the water, which is clean enough at this point to be safe to wade in.

to restore is just a vision of place that has been lost. Many of the urban waterfront projects landscape architects work on are catalyzed by a desire of the city's inhabitants to restore a positive sense of being at the water's edge that many cities have lost over the past hundred years. Stapleton, the old Navy Homeport site on Staten Island, was one of these projects, which illustrates thinking about restoration at multiple scales. We were restoring clean water, restoring memory of historical uses of the site. We were also restoring the connection between the water and the rest of the city.

Since industrialization, many riverfronts the world over have been stripped of their significance as waterfronts. The marginal uses that were relegated to waterfront sites a century ago—factories, hospital isolation wards, and psychiatric facilities—were, at least in New York City, divided from the rest of the city by major highways built to speed people in and out of the city from the suburbs. From the 1960s until only recently, low-income housing was added to the uses pushed to this undesirable edge of the city. In recent decades parking, big-box retail, and other non-water-dependent uses have managed to land on the waterfront, despite a growing appreciation for the value of waterfronts as recreational and important civic spaces. The specifics of what made this happen—highways cutting the city off from the waterfront, big-box retail obscuring any connection—may differ, but in most cases these events have undermined the sense of this place as a waterfront where people would want to be. When faced with a project where that sense of place—the sense of a landscape as part of a larger water world, for instance—has been lost, it sometimes helps to start with just the idea of place and see what we can do to restore that. This kind of visioning process may lead to the actual restoration of a riparian landscape. But then again, it may not.

BUILDING ON SENSE OF PLACE

Our visceral relationship with the landscape is like a form of attachment. When I teach architecture students who have no experience with landscape architecture, I give them an assignment to make a model or series of analytical drawings of a landscape of their childhood that holds special meaning for them. You can see the students reconnecting with something powerful and primal; they spend a tremendous amount of time on their work, and when they

Stapleton environmental flows scheme.

are presenting their finished projects they often emphatically describe things about the landscape that they could not represent, such as scents, people, and time. It's almost as if they are describing a beloved family member, and they often describe some of the values that living in that landscape imbued in them: independence for the kids who ventured out into forests behind their subdivision, community for the kids who live in coastal areas that have been threatened or even wiped out. I get a palpable sense of the love these students have for their home landscapes. To connect with, identify with, and feel fiercely protective of a landscape is to be in love.

When we are invited to look at a project in a landscape that is foreign to us, we are often described as "parachuting" into a project. As professionals, we do not necessarily make the kind of connection to the landscape that someone who has been part of it for a long time has made. It is ideal to walk onto a site and be struck by the power, the beauty, the fragility, or just the potential of the place; we fall in love with the landscapes we work in all the time. But we shouldn't confuse our own enthusiasm for a site with its resonance to the people who live there. In any project, it is essential to try to get to know what this landscape means to the people who have lived in the landscape for a long time before we got there. The issue of how people identify with the landscape is something that has been studied for generations in academe but has not necessarily been explicitly built into the design process. Although we may have internalized technological best practices that can make a landscape more green and sustainable, we still need to ask ourselves, "What are the deeper connections we are making here? What is it about this place that makes it, or made it, so precious to people? Or what is it about this place that needs to be reestablished, to restore an identity that resonates with the people who live here?"

When we start any project, we dive into the stuff of the site: what we observe on the site, what we read in reports and surveys. But when trying to arrive at a cohesive understanding of a site, at some point it's useful to put aside for a bit the complex analysis we have been taught to pursue—studies of natural processes, or circulation diagrams, or historical surveys—and just sit with it. Particularly when one feels overwhelmed by all the layers of natural processes, history, programs, and indeed when one worries about getting it right, it is helpful to step back, to ask oneself a question like the one in the

Existing bulkhead,
Stapleton, Staten Island.

Zen practice attributed to the Zen Master Xuefeng, just to stop and sit and ask oneself, "What is it?" Reflecting on the question, we can begin to relax our preconceptions and overthinking of our lives. Rather than trying to sum up and categorize and make a static evaluation of what a place is, we can open all our senses and ask without preconceptions what a place is. Sometimes the answer will be scientific: It is a layered deposition of minerals. But sometimes, rather than reeling off all the data and studies, the answer might be, as in the story of Xuefeng and two visiting monks, "The wind boat, ferrying the moon, floats on the autumn waters." All we can offer is a response, in the moment, and not an answer. The fact is that on a site, the response to "What is it?" changes constantly. Not only does a place change from one time of day to another, from one season to another, it also changes depending on who is standing in it. The response to the question "What is it?" will shift many times over time. Just as the question of "Restore this landscape to which time in its history?" makes us understand that there is not one right answer, the question of "And just what is this landscape?" makes us understand that there are myriad answers. It's our job to understand how changeable the response is but then also to respect the ephemeral as well as the more enduring responses.

When we ask, "What is the nature of this place?" we can sometimes settle on a response that will drive an entire project. Olmsted did this when he moved from Central Park, an internalized cosmos of many independent and interconnected parts, to design Riverside Park, threaded along the powerful and dramatic Hudson River. "This place is an overlook," he concluded, and the entire design followed to reinforce his reading of this place. A network of walking paths and pull-offs at the carriage road, Riverside Drive, orients you over and over to the river. Riverside Park has become much more—recreation park, dog park, with a buried rail line and a linear garden—but that governing concept, that elemental take on the place, still reads clearly throughout.

The practice of tapping into the elemental nature of a place is not divorced from issues of sustainability or stewardship. A critical task for a designer or anyone in safeguarding the environment is to tap into the qualities that make a place like no other, to pay close attention to sense of place.

In restoration, we often fix on one particular reading of the site, to reestablish a sense of place, or a system, or a community. The question of what that reading is can be pragmatic: What is the most ecologically healthful composition for this site that will be sustainable over the long term? Or the question can be poetic, engaging with resonances that are hard to quantify:

What is the memory of this place that the people who will be using it would most want to identify with?

To redesign the waterfront at Stapleton in Staten Island, which had once been mudflats, was then a small but bustling commercial port, and most recently was fenced in and paved over as the Navy port, we knew that the project needed to restore the place as an accessible waterfront. But *waterfront* can mean many things and take many forms, so we needed to work through a process of defining just what waterfront could mean to make this the best possible place.

Clients often ask designers to prepare three or more alternative schemes when proposing a landscape design for a site. Many designers hate this. We often would just like to barrel ahead and pursue the one design that in our initial studies we think is right. When the contract says three alternatives, as it did at Stapleton, we often busy ourselves preparing two more schemes in addition to the one we think the client should pick, just to satisfy the contract. We secretly favor one scheme not in order to be single-minded but because we often fall in love with the designs we are making. We can feel unduly invested in the one scheme that came to us first.

But the requirement of preparing alternatives for the clients and community to review actually can help the team—which includes the designers, clients, and community—arrive at a solution that feels right to a

The "sublime" scheme, relief at the edge of the city.

majority. For the Stapleton waterfront, in the most nonurban of all New York City's boroughs, the client and community requested three schemes in the concept phase of the project. We developed a "green scheme," a design that expressed environmental flows on the site, a lush, vegetated landscape that brought the immersive feel of Staten Island's Greenbelt out to the waterfront. We developed a "working waterfront" scheme, a gritty landscape of big, open planes, like a boatyard, with lots of room for activities.

And finally, we developed a "sublime" scheme, an open landscape with beach-like arms, where you could just feel the relief of getting out to the edge of the city. My teammates and I all assumed that the "green scheme" would be the preferred alternative, Staten Island being one of the "greenest," or most vegetated, boroughs and sustainability being so front and center at the time, in 2005.

But the client, the Economic Development Corporation, and the community, which historically had resisted projects that promote an urban aesthetic, selected the "working waterfront" scheme. Although new housing and commercial projects on Staten Island in the past have looked decidedly suburban, when it came to this particular waterfront, the community favored a landscape design that drew on the history of shipping, boatyards, and industries such as an old brewery that used to inhabit the site.

If we had just gone ahead and developed a scheme all about environmental flows, we would have missed an opportunity to create something very specific to this place, and for these people who have taken it on themselves to steward its renewal. The final design attempted to restore this waterfront as a vital, active place, as it had been from the earliest days of New York, until it was cordoned off by the Navy in the 1980s.

The "working waterfront" scheme.

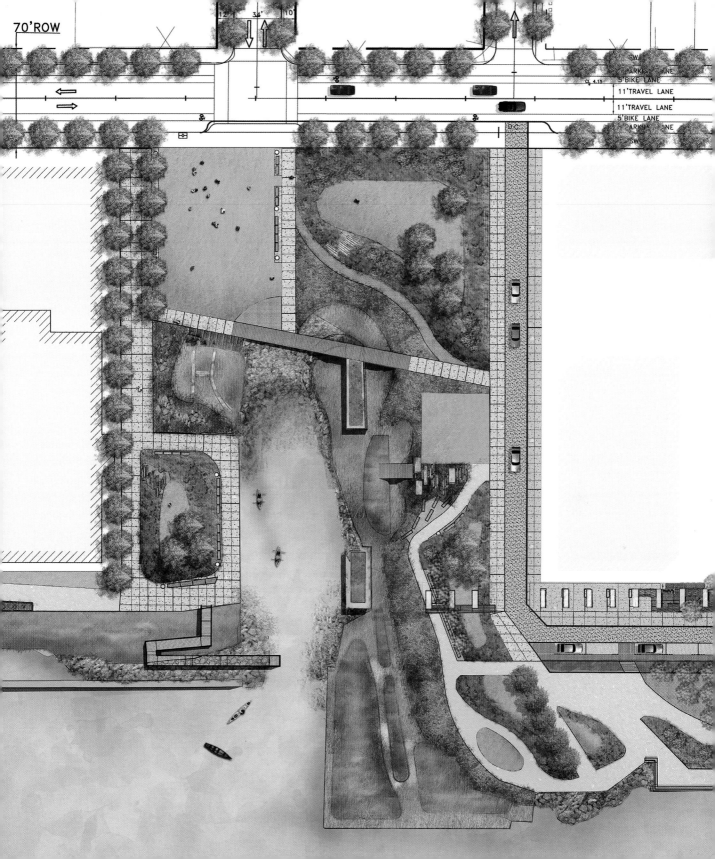

70'ROW

12' 34' 10'

5' BIKE LANE
11' TRAVEL LANE
11' TRAVEL LANE
5' BIKE LANE
PARKING LANE
SW

The restoration of the waterfront included a measure of ecological restoration. We wanted to work with the tidal conditions on the site, constructing a new cove with tidal wetland. As a matter of course, there are certain landscape types we promote for restoration, not strictly for the

The cove would provide a place for kayaking and boatbuilding.

project itself but for the impact large-scale restoration will have on the larger ecosystems of the region. Tidal wetlands reduce flooding, process the largest amount of carbon of any landscape type, cleanse water, and promote biodiversity—this is just for a start. So if I restore a small area of wetland, then my neighbor does a bit more, then others do even more, the net benefit to the region, and the planet, will grow.

But the driver for the Stapleton project remained this working waterfront model, despite our wetland agenda. We incorporated tidal wetlands into a working waterfront, with a small craft launch, and a boat-building school upland. We may not have arrived at this working waterfront wetland solution had we pushed our initial concept of environmental flows. So before we even get our tracing paper out, before we have any meetings, before we visit any sites, we need to try to disabuse ourselves of our preconceptions, our ideas about what a place is, who the people are who live there, and what they will want. The process of meeting, walking together, setting out all the information we can get our hands on, hearing from the many people whose lives will be affected by a project—this process can take us in directions we never expected. So before we even think our first thought, we need to check our preconceptions at the door.

Keeping old, existing wooden pilings in place and infilling with wetland plants. At a hearing an art commissioner asked, "Why did you decide to use such a rustic treatment at the water's edge?" "Because it's there" was the only answer I could think of. Working around existing structures was not yet something seen every day in urban landscape design. It is much more common now.

Reconceiving the whole of central Trenton, New Jersey as a complex of ecological, recreational, and cultural parks.

Restoring Whole Cities

Trenton Capital Parks, Trenton, New Jersey

The Living Water Park was a demonstration of river restoration. Trenton, New Jersey provided an opportunity to go a step farther. When the team I was leading at Wallace Roberts & Todd (WRT) entered the competition to redesign the downtown of Trenton, New Jersey, from the State House to the Delaware and the Assunpink Creek, the brief was to restore connections: the connection between city and river, between neighborhoods, and between contemporary Trenton and its history.

Downtown Trenton right to the waterfront, as it existed for decades, was a sea of parking lots for commuting state workers.

The old Route 29 running
right along the river.

The City of Trenton had been cut off from the water by highways, and a sea of parking lots had rolled out over the years to accommodate the thousands of state workers who commute in from the suburbs. Few people identify Trenton as the site of some of the most important battles of the American Revolution, historically a thriving manufacturing city where ceramics kilns lit up the riverfront. Trenton grew up in an efflorescence of art and industry that yielded, among other treasures, the American ceramics movement and the Roeblings, designers of the Brooklyn Bridge. So when we won the competition to redesign this central district as the New Jersey Capital Parks, we began to delve into the many layers of history and to focus on the historic sites as part of the continuum of arts and crafts traditions in the city.

The main formal move, however, removing the acres and acres of parking and bridging the chasm between the Delaware River and the city's streets, was to restore the connection between the river and the city that had long been lost. Like so many cities in the United States and the world over, a fast-moving highway had cut the city off from the river. The Delaware is a powerful force that floods regularly, and it was kept at arm's length by armored retaining walls and other hard flood control measures, which we recognize now probably increased volume and velocity. By bringing the riparian landscape back onto the site and by bringing access back to the river, we could restore Trenton as a river city. We could also restore Trenton as a great place to work, recreate, and live.

The new park restores the connection between city and river.

Moving the highway upland, and bringing it down to grade, makes room for an appropriately grand park space for the State House, facing the water.

CREATING NEW LIVING SPACES

This design for the new Capitol Green integrates the need for a formal, ceremonial lawn, for events, with the history of the water courses on the site—the darker green representing a subsurface wetland fed by an old buried spring—with the tradition of artists working on public sites in New Jersey. The areas underneath the lines of trees, each one a particularly beloved New Jersey species, are lined with benches designed by local New Jersey artists. The design transforms the space from parking field to a new living space for the city, for big events or for working people looking for a shady place to eat their lunch.

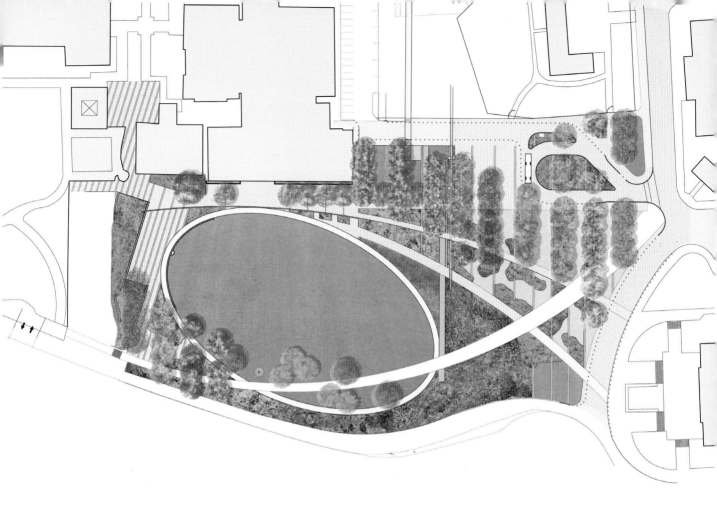

The water from an old, buried creek will be let out to run through a linear grove of native trees, into a constructed wetland that surrounds the great lawn.

In this project we were interested in bringing the art aspect back to the forefront of our agenda. But rather than seeing the main driver of the project being our own artistic expression, we felt more like catalysts, orchestrators, and curators. We wanted to include local artists and artisans as well as historic forms in the design process. The green practices are integrated here as a matter of course. While we were restoring the riverfront and restoring the natural flow of a buried spring within the site, we were also restoring the traditions of art and craft that originally made Trenton one of the premier river cities in the young nation.

REPRESENTING A VISION

The recasting of Trenton as a waterfront city was triggered by a New Jersey Department of Transportation project to move the major roadway that cuts the city off from the water, slightly inboard, to allow for a waterfront park. Route 29 runs across the Assunpink Creek; the view below shows how four of the spans that support the roadway would be retained after the roadway is demolished, and refitted as green, garden-like pedestrian bridges to link the park with the new residential neighborhood to the south. The hard seawalls would be replaced with armored, vegetated slopes. Integrating the river systems, the changes in topography, and the many different uses, making connections between various neighborhoods, linking the historic sites, developing new riparian habitat—all of this comes together in a landscape that both makes distinctions and coheres. We chose to represent the idea in a drawing that looks more like a painting, done by Tobiah Horton at WRT, rather than a more realistic-seeming perspective. The team, and the client, saw this restoration project as an opportunity to restore the artistic spirit that resided in Trenton since its beginnings.

This painterly drawing may have helped win the competition.

RECONNECTING CITY AND RIVER

This design for downtown Trenton between the State House and the Delaware River recasts Trenton as a great place to live, to work, and to visit. The landscape spans different neighborhoods—the Capitol Complex, a new residential neighborhood to the south—and environments, from the urban fabric of State Street and beyond to the riparian corridor running along the Delaware and up the Assunpink Creek. The design pulls the landscape together but also provides distinct spaces for people to engage in the life of the city and the river. The Capitol Green at the center provides a new living room for the city, a series of riverfront terraces bring people out to the river's edge, and a lush river's edge creates a zone for riverine habitat. Reconnecting the life of the city with the life of the river, restoring this vital connection, is central not only to this project but to the majority of the most important urban projects of the past 20 years.

This project, like so many urban park projects of the late twentieth and now the early twenty-first century, tells a story of how cities grow along, and then outgrow, their rivers. The river that originally made life and commerce possible here eventually became the back door of the city. Factories that used water in their manufacturing process chose the riverfront for their plants; they could then dump their dirty water, and other liquid and nonliquid waste, back into the river. But when, in the late twentieth century, urban habits started to change and people started to go outdoors more and drive less, urban dwellers began to see the river as a great place for recreation and contemplation—for parks, in other words. In the 1980s funding for waterfront projects ramped up, through Superfund cleanup projects and via community groups represented by elected officials, trying to redress having been cut off from their waterfronts. So for more than 30 years we have been trying to restore this connection between our cities and their rivers. Bans on pollution have resulted in a resurgence of urban fisheries, with some urban waterbodies such as New York's inner harbor returning to almost swimmable water quality. The waterfront park has become the Central Park of our time— the blue lungs, so to speak, if Central Park functions as the green lungs of the city, the safety valve that returns us to the natural processes we have so often forgotten in our upland lives. It is the place where we can feel fresh air and get our feet wet in the increasingly clean water.

Restoration very strictly defined means reestablishing a specific process or set of processes. More broadly defined it means reviving, bringing back to life, making whole again, or at least making less broken. It can simply mean restoring a use that has been lost. When I was in graduate school, I came across a contemporary Italian design project that was classified as a restoration of a Roman market that had existed on the site. Yet the new landscape bore little resemblance to the historic landscape. It was a modern composition, almost like a modern abstract painting. From this I learned that restoration does not necessarily require us to make an exact replica of what has been lost, not that we could ever actually achieve an exact replica, even if we wanted to. Restoration can mean reignition of a spirit. It can mean retrieving lost uses, such as a market, without reconstructing the original. In landscape, restoration means, in one way or another, a return to life.

Chapter 4:

Conservation

If the task of restoration can be mistakenly thought to require a less than vivid imagination, conservation can seem even less creative. Whereas *restoration* usually implies rebuilding, taking something back to its original state, *conservation* implies safeguarding, preserving a site or portion of a site in its current state, preventing change. In Ian McHarg's *Design with Nature*, one of the key purposes of the overlays of vegetation, slope, hydrology, and so on was to identify the areas that should be off-limits, cordoned off, kept in conservation. Conservation signified a hands-off approach. But conservation can engage the design process in meaningful ways. The delineation of areas for conservation requires planning and design thinking. The principles of conservation—to use little, to minimize waste, to safeguard a landscape that is at risk—can be thoroughly integrated into the design process.

In McHarg's method, the overlays of different natural systems tell you both where the landscape is diverse or fragile, and should be kept free of development, and where the landscape has been most disturbed, and therefore often should be the site for development. Just because you have identified an area for conservation does not mean you can cordon it off and forget about

Shillim retreat was conceived in response to spreading development in the Western Ghats of Maharashtra, India. Looking beyond the project limit is essential for beginning to think about conservation.

it. It would be irresponsible to say that an area is in conservation without understanding the ecological state of the landscape. You have to understand the forces at work—erosion, the role of invasive species, a change in climate, for example—to ascertain whether the area you would like to conserve is likely to remain in its current state with no intervention. Collaborating with ecologists is essential in this process. Very few landscape architects have the training in ecology to be able to sign off on an assessment of ecological health. An ecologist provides the depth of knowledge to judge whether a certain area should be or could be kept in conservation. Once you have had enough help to understand where the landscape is going, you invariably will have to remediate certain conditions; integrating preventive measures with a program or interpretation can constitute a design exercise in itself. A new program inserted into a site will often change drainage patterns; redirecting water to conserve an existing landscape is a creative task and can carry an expressive force.

Conservation means nothing in isolation. You can conserve 1,500 acres of wildlands in the Western Ghats of India, but if habitat is destroyed surrounding it, the area will become an island, and species will decline. Connecting with larger ecosystems is one of the driving principles of conservation: conservation as a global goal, not one defined by the project limits.

Conservation is not about saving individual species. Although we hear about the polar bear or a particular kind of bat, or the decline of certain bee species, anyone working in conservation knows that each species plays a role in a larger system. It is the entire biotic community, or biome, that needs to be safeguarded in order to safeguard individual species, and that biome is part of a much larger web. It is not easy for designers to internalize the science necessary to assess the threat to an ecosystem posed by a particular project or to know the metrics on connectivity or habitat that will make a conservation project meaningful. We work hand in hand with ecologists and other environmental scientists, who can assess the existing situation and make recommendations for measures that will conserve the biome. Year by year, alliances are being formed between scientists and designers. But the ability to work together from day one of a project depends on how well the process is designed and how well team players communicate.

In this era of climate change and mass extinctions, it should be obvious to most people who go into the field of landscape architecture why it is important to include a conservation agenda in our work. But there is conservation and there is conservation. The following series of goals can help designers understand the layering of conservation operations.

Do no harm. Anyone entering the field of landscape design should adopt the landscape version of the physician's mandate. This is not possible on most projects, however. Making changes to the landscape often entails uprooting plants, bulldozing insects and small animals, or displacing people. But we can adopt the most basic of principles, not to use pesticides or herbicides, not to compromise the health of a landscape just to pursue a purely formal interest.

Protect what is there. Conservation measures on a project can be like a tree protection fence, cordoning off areas to be held apart from any new disturbances. Regardless of a project's program, we can recognize biomes in need of protection and forecast that the new program could compromise certain natural systems.

Use less of what is precious. Protecting what is there does not simply mean cordoning off what is fragile. It also means that we conserve resources, whether they are endemic to the site or not.

Desert courtyard,
Casa Finisterra, Baja,
California.

Leave things better than we found them. Determining problems in the way the existing ecological systems function, we can redress some of the problems with our work, reforesting eroded areas, for instance, or slowing water down to reduce erosion.

Link with larger systems and patterns. The larger conservation mandate— to look at the larger ecosystems and assess the potential to connect our project site to larger corridors and biomes—is not just difficult to internalize; we also have no control over surrounding lands and must form alliances with organizations and landholders off the site. Conservation in a vacuum can be meaningless. We can try to conserve species on our site, but unless we join forces with conservation efforts in adjacent landscapes and even regionally, we might expose the landscape we are working on to threats such as disease and invasive species.

Help people value nature as a complex system. Then there is the educational and inspirational component of our work. We can raise consciousness about ecosystems by foregrounding biomes, such as desert or prairie, so that people connect with them and develop a protective attitude.

One of a handful of places
in the world where the desert
meets the sea.

The critical fact to keep in mind is that most designers are not ecologists. We need to partner with people we trust, and who trust us, to do the surveys and make recommendations. We can organize the work into a timeline saying what we are going to do and when, but it will probably be the result of a close collaboration between designers, ecologists, engineers, and other specialists. A case in point is connectivity. We learn about patches and corridors, the principle of creating a connective wildlife corridor between larger areas of habitat. But unless we know how particular creatures move through the landscape, we can't know that just by delineating a link, we will create a successful route between two desired spots. A particular animal may need a route that takes it by a freshwater pool or a source of food that lies outside the direct route we envision. Skilled ecologists can help us make more successful connections to ensure that wildlife will be able to move through larger territories and as a result have more chance of survival and procreation.

Each of the following projects had a different mandate and different process when it comes to conservation. The variety of methods and approaches should suggest that designers never adopt one uniform way of interacting with a site, a client, a design team, or a program.

Casa Finisterra, Baja, California

One of the most photographed and published projects I have worked on—a house compound designed by Steven Harris Architects and Lucien Rees Roberts's interior design—is as much a conservation project as it is a design statement. Noted most often for the way in which it integrates local materials, the native landscape, and modern form, the project promotes an ethic of conservation within a language of high design.

Strictly speaking, the project is not a conservation project; in fact, when we got to the site it had been stripped of vegetation and was just a rocky cliff over the ocean. But the site is in one of the handful of places in the world where the desert meets the sea. It is a landscape that is ecologically rich, and it is strange and beautiful. And spending any time in this landscape, you realize that a desert is not a place with no life; in fact, it is a place where life is starkly, dramatically present.

Blurring the boundaries between surrounding desert and the domestic world.

At points the desert plantings disappear, and the courtyard becomes a sculpture garden, including the mature Washi tree.

The sunlight reflects off the water in a runnel running along the master bathrooms, providing their only source of natural light.

At Casa Finisterra, we wanted to conserve the desert landscape, not in physical fact but in principle. (The site was less than a quarter of an acre hanging over a cliff, so the idea of any large-impact conservation was far-fetched.) We wanted to foreground the desert landscape as a precious, limited resource, composing the landscape in a way that highlights the specificity and beauty of every organism in it. We wanted to challenge the idea that there is a clear boundary between us (people, buildings, institutions) in here and nature (plants, animals, rivers, streams) out there. We wanted to promote the idea of the desert as an appropriate ecology to bring into, or restore to, the domestic world and to conserve in its larger glory.

Almost the entire site, which consisted of sand and rock and one mass of woody plants nestled within them, would need to be cleared to make room for the 3,000-square-foot footprint of the buildings. We could save the rocks and the plants close by, but everything else needed to go. The idea of any restoration would also be inappropriate, because the cliff site was dug out to create a flat plane for the buildings and courtyard, and the plants could not be established in the rock without a lot of irrigation—not to mention the fact that all the surrounding lots were being developed, so restoration would have created a postage stamp of cliffscape surrounded by big fat villas, more a museum than a restoration. So we set about making a completely artificial world that brought the desert landscape into it.

I find that I never apply one of the five strategies in isolation; they all overlap, and particularly so at Casa Finisterra. The attention to detail at Casa Finisterra and the intentional composition of spaces, layout of paving, and placement of plants and objects required intense study in plan and section, in model, and on the site. The necessary level of attentiveness was equal to the care with which we do the most expressive projects, the ones that grade closer to art than to conservation. But the project for me is about conservation of the fragile desert landscape; we wanted to highlight its beauty and richness and create a landscape that would support life. If people did this all over the developing areas of Baja, the value of the desert landscape would be formalized and the native landscape conserved.

Nor is the design process ever pure, especially when it comes to sustainability. Although we wanted initially to handle all the stormwater on-site through a series of bioswales, the amount of space and the volumes of water in hurricane season made this impracticable. If we had been following best practices we would not have torn up so much of the site; we would have focused on how the landscape could slow water down;

we would have reused the gray water from the house. None of this was practicable given the codes, the costs, and the whole team's vision for the project, including the client's.

I had already designed two landscapes for this client. The Boxwood Farm in western New Jersey drew on regional garden traditions—a cottage garden, water garden, and a pool punctuated by a pool house Steven Harris designed using traditional corn-crib construction—and more formalized agricultural landscapes. For an adobe house compound just outside Santa Fe, I enjoyed bringing some of the technologies used in permaculture—sustainable land use practices pioneered in Australia—into the domestic garden. We designed pumice wick plantings that pull and retain moisture through volcanic rock, creating a flourishing microclimate; I also had long had an ambition to make a mullein garden, showcasing the roadside "weeds" of velvety sagey florets close to the ground that send up tall yellow flower spikes in the summer, and the path down to the hot tub was to become a mullein paradise that I thought would also look beautiful at night, when the leaves take on a silvery shine and the spiky flowers topping out at about eye level would surround you in the dark. The client shifted her sights to the cliffside property in Cabo, so this house was never realized, but I learned a lot from the exercise.

QUESTIONING PURISM

I took our client to visit a permaculture nonprofit, to see whether we could integrate some of their practices into the project. I prepared for the meeting by skimming a book on their demonstration garden, which showcases the entire permaculture lexicon: Contour swales retain water; plantings on the swales' berms prime water up into the soil, improving the growing matrix for plants; organic orchards and gardens produce food; and chickens scarify and fertilize the soil, also improving its fertility. My quite game client and I sat at a long conference table while the head of the organization ran through all these practices, and the head designer showed us photographs. Toward the end of their description, the designer said, "Of course you won't need a lot of chickens for a property of that size, just maybe three or four."

I looked at my client, whose poker face is legendary.

"I am afraid," I told the designer "that my client will not be able to keep chickens, as this is a second home, and they will be away for long periods

of time." This could have been irrelevant, because there would be a house watcher who would have been able to feed the chickens and change their water. But I knew without having to ask that my client was just not interested in keeping chickens. She had enough to manage, and although she was open to following me down this permaculture path, I knew she would have limits.

"It's not permaculture if you don't have chickens," the head designer told me.

"This isn't a demonstration, we just wanted to try to integrate some of the xeriscaping [landscaping with plants that don't need a lot of water] practices. We are already using pumice wicks, but I wanted to know if you might be able to work with us to provide more recommendations for sustainable practices."

The head designer started to squirm in his chair.

"There's no point in adopting some of the practices if others are just going to negate them."

"I don't think failure to raise chickens on the property will negate all of the positive water harvesting and native planting moves."

"The earth will not be scarified."

"I'm sure if you made a recommendation for manual scarification, my client would follow it."

"But that would be a waste," he said to us, two people who wanted to try to make things a little better, to offset new development, albeit only partially, by more responsible landscape practices. Our projects rarely can follow the kind of purism that permaculture follows. If a client asked us to do something closed-loop, self-sustaining and operating on every level as well as it could, most of us would jump at the chance. But the conditions to allow this to happen are rare.

"There are going to be many components of this landscape that will appear wasteful to a purist, but this is the program for my client. For instance, there's going to be a hot tub at the bottom of the mullein garden."

The head designer just looked at me. This was beyond the pale, a hot tub on a project that was using permaculture practices.

"I have another meeting. Very nice to meet you," the head designer explained as he shook our hands and exited stage left.

The program called
for appropriate desert
plantings cheek-by-jowl
with luxury amenities.
This struck a number of
purists as untoward.

The top of the steps down to the house from the road.

The existing rocks were planted with species found growing outside the site.

The view out to the sea.

Entry into a compressed
gateway to the compound.

Descending into
the desert landscape.

Passing through the entry
pavilion into the courtyard.

View of sea beyond
the courtyard.

Nearing the edge of the cliff,
and the outdoor living room.

The top of the steps down
to the study and pool.

View down to the pool
and sea from the steps.

View back up the steps
to the courtyard.

The pool rests between
two walls, one concrete.
the other natural stone;
the view to the sea is
momentarily obscured.

The wall seems to be
the only thing sepa-
rating the pool water
from the sea water.

During the whales' migration you can watch from the
perch at the end of the pool, where the boundary
between it and the sea almost disappears.

When we make a garden now, in this second wave of ecological design, we first look at the larger site systems, patterns of vegetation, water, sun and wind, for instance. We now as a matter of course make connections between the landscape that we are intervening in and the surrounding landscape. In a resort area like this southern tip of Baja, California, the traditional courtyard acted as an oasis, where palms, bananas, and other tropical plants were fed and irrigated to create a lush refuge from the harsh desert environment. The architects followed this tradition in one sense, arraying the building in bars surrounding a void space, bucking the more recent resort trend of building a rambling pile in the middle of the site, leaving precious little space around it. But we broke with the landscape tradition of oasis in a major way, bringing the plants and creatures of the desert into the house compound.

We wanted to make a legible connection between the desert and the domestic world for a number of reasons: to provide a habitat link for the birds, lizards, rodents, and other desert residents; to bring the sense of being in the desert, which attracted the clients to this area in the first place, into the architecture of the compound; and to blur the boundary between inside and outside, reversing the age-old habit of creating a gated, almost fortified compound in a harsh environment.

The way in which we used desert plants also broke with a recent convention. In the years before we started on this project, landscape designers had begun to use plant species found in the desert, but they often deployed them in patterns they imported from different design traditions, using them in broad swaths such as you would see in an English garden, and mulching them with pebbles or sand. But the desert landscape supports life on the groundplane, with a low datum of grasses and other plants that offer food and cover. We wanted to create a layered habitat, using plants that grow low to the ground as well as the taller specimens of plumeria and cactus that one has come to expect in the region.

OBSERVING

Plants do not occur in the desert in obviously predictable patterns or numbers. If the broad swaths of plantings in the English landscape tradition represent abundance, the idiosyncratic occurrences of plants in the desert represent opportunity: A confluence of favorable conditions and events has allowed that particular plant, for instance, to germinate, take root, and survive in this very specific matrix of soil, rock, or sand. We spent many hours

Barrel cactus in the courtyard.

out in the heat, mapping the way plants occurred, sitting and listening to the birds and the flies and experiencing so many other forms of life. We had to steep ourselves in the landscape, or rather bake ourselves, to begin to understand how life happens there.

We wanted to recreate that sense of serendipity, not to say adversity, in the Casa Finisterra landscape. The eye moves over this landscape differently, and the feeling of being in this landscape is different. Once you acclimatize, the landscape is quite immersive, lush even. Living. Because we included plantings at the several layers of grasses, cactus, broadleaf plants, birds, and other desert organisms made it their home fairly quickly. I received a call from the client soon after she arrived for her first extended visit after construction. She didn't talk about swimming in the pool or eating overlooking the sea. She talked about the orioles she was watching alighting on branches less than 10 feet from where she sat.

A green roof in a desert environment may look quite different from the sedum roof we have come to expect. This roof in Cabo acts as a green roof, over occupied space, but extends the desert landscape over the top of the building.

LOOKING AT EVERY PROJECT WITH FRESH EYES

In this area of Baja, the intense aridity is punctuated by torrential rains, particularly in the hurricane season. The entry to the compound reflects the flow of water over stone: All the upland stormwater flows through the channel at the base of the retaining wall, at the right, and the holes in the paving where the mortar has been left out allow water to flow into a trench drain.

Many components of the design were intended to slow water down, promote a native palette that would attract wildlife, and reposition the desert landscape as the landscape to showcase and promote in a residential project in this region, as opposed to a lush, irrigated oasis of palms. Just promoting this vision can have an impact on conservation: It elevates the desert as worthy foreground and promotes xeriscape plantings, which have less impact on groundwater than tropical plantings and keep humidity levels low, so less air conditioning is needed (air conditioning is used to lower humidity, in addition to temperatures). By breaking with the convention of landscaping that turns the focus inward from the desert and creates an irrigated fantasy, we can turn the focus back out to the desert as a precious, rich landscape to conserve.

One of the biggest challenges in this kind of assignment is how to bring the desert landscape and the domestic world together, without making it look like a mess of unruly plants or a museum of desert plants, plants so isolated they look as if they are on display.

The gaps between paving stone were left unmortared over a trench drain that carries water from uphill out through the courtyard.

Concrete pavers were run around existing boulders; the concrete was tinted the color of the stone.

The steps down to the pool were detailed with concrete, sand, and stone to feel embedded in the cliff.

The landscape needed to look like part of the desert but clearly inhabited. This would require a tremendous amount of attention. Sometimes things just happen, such as the juxtaposition of the boulder and paving on page 149. Existing rock outcrops and boulders were left in place, with paving scribed around them. But the photo at left also shows how the new landscape was integrated visually into the language of the desert environment: The sand used in the stabilized stone-fine paving was taken from the site, so it is actually the same material and color as the rock. If untreated concrete had been used, the stark white of the concrete would have contrasted sharply with the warmer, rosy-colored stone, so the concrete used for paving was tinted the same color. Many small decisions create the sense that this landscape is of a piece.

So many decisions make this image very specific to this place: the selection of local stone; the color of the concrete, tinted to match the stone; the narrow width of the pool coping, which intensifies the connection between the pool and the ocean; the color of the pool's interior, which makes the pool water the same color as the sea. None of these would show up on a checklist, but the result is a place that feels a part of the landscape from which it emerges. Conserving the landscape can mean more than just preserving it. Expressing the qualities of the place and elevating them to a level where people will see them anew and appreciate them all the more is an act of conservation. This is why I placed Casa Finisterra in the "Conservation" chapter of this book: It is not a restoration. It is a representation of the desert landscape in a highly artificial framework. It is a design that promotes conservation but in no way replicates a desert biome. It is a small patch of a special landscape that we hoped would engender more, and it has. The norm in new developments and luxury housing in many parts of the world—and the team on this project can't claim credit for this, we are all touched by the zeitgeist—has become to float new buildings within the larger matrix of native plants. Small projects lead to bigger movements.

Minimizing Our Impact

Shillim Retreat and Institute, Maharashtra, India

This landscape in India, in the Western Ghats between Mumbai and Pune, is hot and desert-like in the summer, but during the monsoon season it becomes a water landscape. The Shillim retreat and institute, a combination of a luxury retreat and an institute for learning, is sited within 2,500 acres of land that ranges from high butte to rice fields. The design negotiates between the intense conditions of drought in the summer and inundation during the monsoon; a small number of plants can adapt to both, and the huge volumes of water flowing down to the central nallah, or drainage way, at the valley floor, must be accommodated. The client had visited this region since childhood and wanted to conserve a significant patch of the dramatic and ecologically rich landscape, as the surrounding land is eyed for development and pieces picked off, to be fenced and irrigated.

The program includes spa resort amenities, including recent additions to the resort menu of a spiritual retreat and organic farming. At the heart of the valley, we sited an institute for the exchange of ideas and information relating to sustainable development. Shillim Institute provides space for conferences and workshops, arts, cooking, and other practices, all filtered through the lens of sustainability. The Shillim Foundation is a global body that promotes work that pushes the concept of conservation into a new era, where conservation does not look simply to ecology but also to the arts—music, performance, painting, and ceramics—as an integral component. The mission of the retreat, the institute, and the foundation, conserving resources, has come to mean cultural resources as well.

The site rests within a bowl, defined by a crescent of high ridges. The many and varied geological stratifications create a landscape of ridges, buttes, benches, and plateaus. The forest that has grown sheltered within the bowl is rich and diverse. The tradition of grazing animals and clearing trees for fuel caused tremendous erosion during the monsoons; by the time we started on this project, in 1997, much of the upland soil had washed down into the valley floor, and there was almost no groundwater, because all the monsoon rains ran rapidly over the eroded soils and down into the flat terraces surrounding the main nallah, depositing a deep soil matrix for rice farming.

The 2,500-acre site sits in a bowl surrounded by high ridges and buttes. A diverse forest occupies the heart of the site.

The savanna as it appeared in 1997, when the team first visited the site.

Cliffs along the high ridge.

I was brought to the project by Steven Harris, the architect on Casa Finisterra and the Boxwood Farm. He had been asked by Vrinda Khanna, a young architect practicing in New York and Mumbai, and a former student of his from Yale, to join her in developing a master plan for what was then a 1,500-acre site up in the Western Ghats. Harris asked me to join him. The fact that I was brought in before planning had begun was at the time unusual; more often the landscape planner, designer, or architect would be brought in after all the buildings were sited, to "landscape" the place—the "parsley around the pig" approach, in the worst cases.

But Harris had come to recognize that landscape architects often understand things architects don't: topography, issues of circulation that have a huge impact on the way the landscape unfolds, and most importantly ecological moves such as maintaining and creating wildlife corridors and habitat patches. We traveled to Shillim together in 1997, to walk the site, meet with the client, and start to plan. Little did I know at the time that it would take the team—and not just a team consisting of us but an amoebically organizing and reorganizing team of consultants from the world over—the next 10 years to finalize a long-term plan for what grew in those years to 2,500 acres.

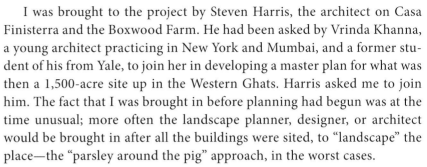

Rice fields on the valley floor.

The monsoon rains persist as late as November in the nallah, or waterway, at the bottom of the valley floor.

The rice fields are separated by berms; water flows from one to another via a series of sluices. The trees grown on the berms are generally fruit trees such as mango and jack fruit.

Rice fields near the end of monsoon season.

The forest is nestled below the high ridges and buttes, midway up the 200-meter elevation change from valley floor to ridge.

The team spent countless hours walking the site, developing the dispersal method of planning for the many different parts of the program. The team included engineers and horticulturists, as well as architects and landscape architects.

DRAWING A LINE IN THE SAND

We worked with a team of local ecologists to understand the composition and assess the health of the forests, ravines, and plains. We walked and studied the surveys and spent many hours discussing the merits of different areas of the site for different programs, nestling some buildings up near the benches, others on the savanna. The ecologists made our job much simpler when we met to develop an approach to all the various habitats: The lead ecologist took the plan and drew almost a straight line that separated the forested and steeply sloped areas that were intact from the disturbed lower slope and valley. No development would occur from the lowest line of the forest all the way to the ridges; this zone not only contains diverse plant communities but also harbors many wildlife species, including barking deer and the occasional big cat. Any fantasies about small, delicate structures within the forest area or anywhere upstream, so to speak, had to be abandoned.

At the same time, we were getting to know the economic advisors, who were looking out for the commercial interests of the development. They told us we needed to cluster the entire program in one spot, definitely including a highrise holiday hotel with an arcade and restaurant on the rooftop. This was the resort convention, and in fact the developer convention, of the era: Concentrate the program in one spot to economize on the services you offer and the associated infrastructure. We argued that we wanted to disperse the program over a larger area, to take advantage of the diverse landscapes and to ensure that being out in the landscape would be an integral part of one's stay. We also argued that in this region, people walk long distances with no problem. Once I ran out of film all the way at the top of the butte, and my companion from the village offered to hike what for me was a 2-hour distance back down to the camp; he returned within 1 hour.

Regardless of our arguments to the contrary, the advisors persisted in claiming we needed to aggregate all the development in one area. The zone we had assumed would be developed occupies a roughly 200-acre area that included the savanna-like plateau, the eroded slopes below, and the rice fields at the valley floor. The area we had identified is arrayed on at least three different levels, in long bench-like fingers. There was no way to lay out the entire program in this area, because the grade changes were too severe. We countered that if we needed to site all the program in one place, we needed a contiguous site large enough. So we moved the entire development to the other side of the valley, to a plateau that I had always thought was in some way unfavorable: Few tree species grew there, it was in the shadow of the ridges much of the day, and there was something about the way air did not circulate there that made me feel it was unhealthy. This sense was borne out when our horticulturist visited, and on seeing where we had moved the whole development, was horrified. To move the resort to what she considered the worst area of the entire landscape was shocking to her. I felt differently, and I explained that sometimes we want to build on the best areas of the landscape at hand, but then we have to do a huge amount of work to ensure that we do not mess it up. Fallingwater in any architect's hands other than Frank Lloyd Wright's might have been a blight on a beautiful ravine. But if we have a big project where we will have to regrade, replant, and create new waterbodies, we might actually be able to transform an unhealthy place into a healthy one. By recontouring the land, we can redirect water flow and also encourage better air flow. Importing better soils from elsewhere on the site (such as the valley, where rice fields need to be regraded periodically), topdressing with compost, can have a huge impact on the way a landscape works, so new plantings will thrive and improve the environment by scrubbing the air, filtering water, and attracting new wildlife.

DISPERSING THE PROGRAM

Patience, perseverance, and sometimes a little bit of luck are needed when working on planning projects with so many goals and agendas. Often we are told that something we think is the right thing to do is off the table. In this case we just needed to wait it out. One look at the infrastructure costs (the road alone was a big-ticket item) for siting the program across the valley from the more accessible yet less contiguous site and we were back where we wanted to be, at the heart of the landscape. What had evolved as a project revolving around conservation would have had to spend a tremendous amount of energy regenerating a part of the site that, for some reason, had failed to thrive.

The different program components, here a spa villa, were dispersed throughout the site, each conceived by the architect to draw on the character of the landscape around it.

The village guest rooms are barely visible from the rice fields in the valley.

The village guest rooms are partly cut into the earth; gabions holding back the soil are planted with species that can survive in intense drought but also tolerate the monsoons.

We could disperse the buildings over the approximately 200 acres of disturbed lands on the plateau and slopes grading down into the valley floor, close by the small village of Bodchilwadi. Not only would this keep the new building from fragile, ecologically rich systems, it also could remediate some of the degradations that had gone before. New construction was accompanied by contour trenching and reforestation.

The result is a large number of small footprints, rather than a small number of large footprints; a restored forest with a new program, as opposed to a new program in an existing forest.

The relaxation center was sited within a mango grove on a slope overlooking the rice fields and spa zone.

The developed area, with the exception of the spiritual retreat, is bounded by the lower plateaus, avoiding the ecologically fragile forest and the deeper ravines, which harbor many forms of life. With the simple line drawn by the local ecologists, we safeguarded many hundreds of acres of diverse forest.

The newly grown forest has grown up to meet the forest suites. When you can't put the building in the forest, you can grow a new forest to meet the building.

We minimized the visual impact of the new construction on the valley by breaking the program up into small chunks. We sited all the buildings on-site, by hand. Believe it or not, some designers will draw a footprint on a plan, and the contractor will lay the structure out on the site and just build it. A better way to do it is to stand on the site with the drawings, look for places where you can avoid major trees and watercourses, put flags in the ground where you want the buildings to go, get the flags surveyed, and make any adjustments to avoid significant trees or patches.

The gatehouse was sited on the slopes; the clean lines of the edging and gravel create an ordered foreground to the wilder valley beyond.

The club, the social center of the retreat, during the dry season.

The club just after the monsoon season.

The gatehouse nestled into the reforested slopes. The club, the social center of the retreat, was sited around an existing mango on the bench halfway up the lower slopes below the savanna.

SLOWING WATER DOWN

Measures to reduce erosion and recharge groundwater were begun in 2003. Gulley plugs, check dams, and contour trenches slowed the water flow, allowing it to percolate down into the ground.

Starting around 2006, residents observed a reduced volume of water flowing into the main nallah on the valley floor.

The small nallahs were plugged with check dams, which slowed the water down.

Working on the site at Shillim in the summer, when temperatures can reach 40 degrees Celsius, can lead one to believe that there is no stormwater problem at Shillim. But planning and design have to take into account changes in the stormwater flows that new uses, new roads, and new plantings will create. Swales and trenches must be sized in order to be able to accommodate the enormous volumes of water flowing down from the ridges during the monsoon season.

Thousands of meters of contour trenches were dug, to detain the water and promote the growth of vegetation. The lowered velocity of the water and the opportunity for growth created by the trenches resulted in massive revegetation over the space of 4 or 5 years. The volumes of water running into the lower nallah were reduced visibly.

The siting and restoration approach built on the different landscape types, drawing on each for architectural and landscape character. The spa was sited within the rice fields, with a main building acting almost as a dam. The lead architect, Steven Harris, conceived of a building that acts both as architecture and as infrastructure.

The gatehouse courtyard was designed around an existing tree; leftover Shahabad stone was crushed to make the gravel surface.

COLLABORATING

From a design perspective, architects Steven Harris and Tom Zook were not entirely focused on what the buildings would look like but on what the views of the site would be once the buildings were built. Shillim is seen as a place where you go to be out in the landscape, not the kind of place where the room fittings and spa treatments are the marketing handle. The rooms were intended to be spare, and the restorative treatments focused on mind, body, and spirit, not just body. A series of hikes and climbs are the staple activity for visitors, taking you up through the forest, along the ridges, onto the high benches, and down through the valley. The walks take you through culturally significant sites, such as sacred ficus groves and the village temple. When siting 100 rooms, a club, a spa, a spiritual retreat, and a riding center, not to mention the back-of-house and staff quarters, Harris worried from the outset

Shillim spa villa.

that the scale of these buildings would ruin the landscape. The massive roof-scapes would blow out the scale of the valley.

His office did study upon study of how buildings could be configured to minimize their impact on the landscape—not to disappear, to be read clearly as architectural forms, but somehow to mediate their own scale within the valley. He and his associate Tom Zook arrived at a roof treatment—a faceted series of planes, seemingly floating above the volume of the building—that looks light and breaks down the scale of the building.

The formal rules Steven Harris and Tom Zook established for the architecture were built on faceted roofs that would break down the scale of the structures in the context of the valley.

MAINTAINING A STRONG DESIGN LEAD

The resulting architecture fits snugly into the landscape, preserving views and conserving the forests, ravines, and high ridges that have drawn people to this region for ages. The process that made this possible was an intensively collaborative one, in which we spent many days walking the site together. The first 3 years we were working on the planning of the project, there were no accommodations on the site, and a driver drove us from Lonavala, an hour and a half away, or Pune, another hour and a half away, every morning and back every night. We spent our days hiking with surveys, discussing different siting strategies, finding new spectacular landscapes and views. At night we would draw up ideas or have planning sessions, trying to come to some sort of consensus. Sometimes the discussions were quite contentious. One September, just as the monsoon was ending, Steven Harris, Tom Zook, and I, along with the team of engineers and architects from the client's side, hiked up to the signature butte at one end of the mountain ridge. It is a 50-foot vertical climb, and the men who had been helping us hike and correlate the surveys to the actual land were there to help us place each foot on the climb up. What we found up there was breathtaking—a rolling grassy plain that felt as if it were floating in the sky—and Harris's reaction was the opposite of mine. Harris took one look at this sublime plateau and said, "This is where the spiritual retreat should go." I winced; the idea of new building up there, along with toilets and food, made me think the specialness of this place would devolve, not just because of the difficulty of construction and the scars it would make, but because the retreat was something I imagined you climbed up to, and there would just be space. The butte was not big enough to site the retreat and leave space where you could get this feeling of the infinite. In addition, the butte looked right down over the intact forest and would bring more people to this side of the site, which was across the line in the sand the local ecologists had drawn. So I told Harris I didn't think this was a good place for the retreat. Luckily we had worked together for many years, and the ensuing hot-tempered argument did not ruin our relationship. Steven had a point: This prominent site had pride of place within the whole ridge, and he could design a building that blended in with the butte. Eventually the client acquired the other end of the ridge, a much bigger series of plateaus, oriented away from the interior of the bowl rather than into it, and moved people through an already disturbed farmland on the way up to the retreat. So the team—actually the client—sited the retreat on that far plateau, about a 2-hour hike from

Spiritual retreat site: in praise of emptiness.

the valley floor. I still had reservations about a building up there; it felt like construction would defile a place we all recognized was sublime. Eventually a no-build fiat won, but not on my argument at all. The construction team determined that it wasn't feasible to take materials and stage construction up that vertical height.

So many activities go into promoting conservation, from literally cordoning areas off to showcasing fragile landscapes. As designers we could not do this on our own; we may think we know enough, but working not just with an ecologist, hydrologist, or other specialist but someone who is local and knows the site and surroundings intimately is going to provide information

Bridge across one of the lower nallahs, below the relaxation center.

and perspective that someone from elsewhere can't possibly know or adopt. We can also offer a perspective that someone local may not have.

The lessons of Shillim have reverberated through all our subsequent work. Sometimes when we are contorting ourselves to do the best job and study the site the best and integrate all of the agendas, it may be that just drawing one line to conserve habitat—you can't touch this—would be the most effective, efficient, and economical way to plan. This was certainly Ian McHarg's method, based on a belief that no matter where we are going to build, we will do damage to the existing environment. Much as we think these days that we are beyond such a binary system, in fact it works in terms of conserving physical resources.

Much more difficult and challenging, however, is to understand how the work you do on any part of the site, fragile or disturbed, can have a deleterious impact on the qualities you want to conserve. Once again scale is our medium, and by responding in a form that would support, and not destroy, the scale of the valley, the architects conserved this unique and sheltered landscape.

Reforestation of the eroded
lower slopes has become
self-perpetuating, creating a
dense forest cover over what
was formerly pastureland.

Chapter 5:

Regeneration

It might seem that the previous strategies can lead to projects that are finished once the designers are done: Queens Plaza has been reinvented, Cabo has been re-desertified. But these projects need ongoing maintenance, and not just the mowing and pruning type. Someone needs to watch as the landscape changes, and there is no landscape on the planet that is not in a perpetual process of change. Even a concrete wall weathers. One of the roles of the designer that is not often made explicit is as agent engaging in the landscape as it grows and changes.

So imagine that you are not just closing the door on a project, you are actually setting processes in motion. You are going beyond just safeguarding existing processes or installing a finished product; you are making the structure, sometimes physical, sometimes social or economic, for the place to perpetuate and regrow itself, not just staying the way it was when you finished your particular project in this landscape but changing over time into something else.

Building into a project the ability not only to maintain but also regrow, we see our roles in a smaller light: We are just facilitating one tiny stage in this landscape's life. But we can actually set processes in motion that will reach well beyond our lives and may still exist long after the physical form we have helped create is gone.

In regeneration, we are helping to set processes in motion that restore or reestablish something that has been lost. However, regeneration differs from restoration in that a regenerative design will not only reestablish the system that was lost but will leave that system in motion, relatively self-sustaining, whether it is a wetland or a market. We plan in all ecological restoration projects for them to regenerate, but in some projects regeneration is the driver.

There exist different modes of regeneration, and most projects need more than one. There is *economic regeneration*, in which education, job creation, and entrepreneurship help make a community more self-sustaining; there is *cultural regeneration*, in which new programs, venues, or rehabilitation efforts spur a renaissance within a community. These often go hand in hand for us with *ecological regeneration*, in which a natural process is set in motion. In all of these, *regeneration* generally refers to a process or action that not only makes a community—urban, ecological, human, animal— more self-perpetuating but also resilient to damage or disturbance.

Creating Jobs

The 2,500 acres of ridge, savanna, forest, and rice terraces of Shillim are also home to a small village at the heart of the valley floor. Over the 10 years it took to plan and design the retreat, the people who lived there were gradually employed, first as guards, guides, assistants to the designers and surveyors, and then as nursery staff. A 15-acre nursery was built starting in 2003 at the edge of the manmade Pawna Lake, outside of the Shillim retreat watershed.

The nursery has raised more than 100,000 plants, most for use in the planting of the site after construction (including many erosion control species) but some for sale in the market to produce additional income for the running of the nursery.

The process of integrating the people who live at Shillim into the operations of the retreat actually began several years before. There had been much skepticism and worry in the village about the ultimate plans for the site. When two staff members charged with developing the horticultural programs

Nursery operations using local propagation methods.

for Shillim helped the people in the village build a small dam, which brought the water source about 100 meters closer to the village, a bridge was made between the staff and the people who live in the village. Now almost all the villagers have a role in the retreat.

Respecting and Reinforcing Community

The community engagement process has been the subject of much study, in recent times from Christopher Alexander and Kevin Lynch to Ann Forsyth. Many organizations that promote certain causes such as social justice have learned over the years that a slow, incremental, and almost invisible process can make great strides in remedying a situation or addressing injustice, whereas the more conventional community process of holding meetings may not be as effective.

In areas where the causes, such as gay rights, would meet with hostility and even violence, this subterranean approach is necessary; momentum is built up one person at a time, as personal relationships, and trust, are built. But even when the cause is not as inflammatory, the more organic, incremental approach can work better than taking boards to a community meeting, presenting what the goals, ideas, or even designs are, getting feedback and integrating it into the plans—or not.

At Queens Plaza, for instance, the project manager had built up many relationships over the 12 or so years she had been present in the area before the project began; many lunches, walks, and phone calls took place long before the official community meetings, which were not that well attended. Over many years of presenting at community meetings, I have also learned

The people who live in the village use the nallah for washing; a new dam built around 2003 moved the water 100 meters or so closer to the village.

to step back when we have encountered a lot of resistance on a particular move, such as removing parking. On many projects—Stuyvesant Cove in New York, or Trenton, or especially Queens Plaza, where many people, especially government employees, parked on the land that was slated to turn into a park—tempers flare, as people feel that they are experiencing a taking. But once we started to ask around and really count the raised voices, we discovered that the group most violently opposed to the removal of parking was a small cell, a minority. The community that shows up at the community meeting may not be the community that is best served. In the case of Stuyvesant Cove, the first phase of work in Trenton, and Queens Plaza, the parking was just removed, no one protested, and the community got a landscape that improved the environmental and economic health of the neighborhood.

The idea that the development team and local residents doing a project together could bridge more differences than holding community meetings does not necessarily translate to all situations. But a planning and design team needs to look at the community and choose the best route.

Leveraging Local Knowledge

The old community meeting model assumes that the consultants have the skills, the community just needs to show up and voice their needs, and the planners will figure out how to incorporate them, or not, into the plans. But if you look at any project more like a cultural exchange than a top-down professional–civilian system, as we did at the Living Water Park, you may find more skills and knowledge than you could have imagined. And doing so will enable your project to contribute to and strengthen local ties long after you have moved on to the next project.

During the desert months at Shillim, when temperatures can reach 110 degrees Fahrenheit and humidity is 0 percent, the people in the village dig down 4 feet under the plateau to retrieve land crabs, which survive on the moisture trapped underneath the surface of the earth. Understanding how to make do with very little, and respecting subsistence living as a sustainable way of life, can have repercussions for visitors when they return to their more technologically advanced home environments. The storehouse of knowledge embodied in the people who have lived in the valley for centuries is one of Shillim's most valuable natural resources. What lessons about sustainable life and every other aspect of life can we learn from this place?

When Steven Harris had designed the signature buildings at Shillim—the club, the spa, the relaxation center—the next task was to design the rest of the buildings: the 100 rooms, the treatment rooms, the back of the house, the riding center, all of the required program beyond the iconic structures. The question was how to respond to the language he and Tom Zook had developed, the broken roof planes and the clear, articulated volumes. Do the buildings draw from that language or contrast with it? The discussions of how this would work and who should design all of these became legendary. Should the client hire one architect, in which case the iconic Steven Harris architecture would stand out, with the other buildings as a kind of background? Or should the client engage other star architects, in which case the whole could become a kind of architectural beauty contest, with all the buildings standing out front. Either one of these had its flaws; the goal was for the whole to be innovative and not formulaic, for Shillim to be an experience of landscape and not to be all about the architecture.

After many of these discussions, Harris had an idea that could avoid the pitfalls: Start an institute, and eventually the mission could be sustainable development, but bring the best architecture students in India and abroad to work on all the subsequent buildings under Harris (whose teaching at Yale has produced a number of star architects) and selected architects from India and elsewhere. The institute, and Shillim, would become a kind of laboratory for architecture that is site responsive but also stellar, integrated with the landscape, environmentally responsive, collaborative—there were so many levels on which an institute would operate to test out and formalize ideas and methods. Eventually the idea went dormant because the need to develop the rest of the architecture quickly and economically took precedence. Architects Robert Schultz and Vrinda Khanna took on the development of the rest of the architecture and the interiors, adding their own sensibility that is both spare and textured.

The idea of the institute did not die, and we worked on it intermittently, writing a mission statement in 2008:

To conserve the natural and cultural heritage of the Western Ghats, and engage the region in the global discussion on sustainability.

The institute would turn what could have been a museum—once the surrounding land is developed, the site could stand as a memorial to a lost landscape—into a place of exchange. By engaging in the conversation about conservation and integrating cultural heritage and sustainability, the institute propels Shillim into the future, offering a new model of hospitality

The Shillim Institute, sited next to the village.

in which the guest can participate in forums, workshops, and performances. The institute set a process in motion that transcends the brief, becoming much more than the sum of its parts. The hope is that the programs of the institute will catalyze a shift in the role of the landscape in local development, to orient new uses to the extremely high value of the native landscape and iconic landforms.

Unbuilt: Renewing a Site's Vitality: Governors Island Competition, New York City

Most of the projects illustrated thus far have been built. However, many times we design projects that never get built. Some of these are competition entries that we didn't win. Others are projects that for some reason, usually financial, were stopped. These projects are instructive on many levels: The more speculative are often testing grounds for us, and when they do not come to fruition parts of them carry into our next projects, pushing the work further while staying within the realm of the feasible. Submitting for a competition is a particularly intense process. The work is intense because deadlines are tight and the amount of work prodigious. It is all-engrossing because the team is being asked to imagine a place that does not exist yet, almost in a vacuum, and package it so that a jury will fall in love with it. You have to fall in love with it a little yourself in order to have the energy to see it through. Not winning is an eye-opening experience. Even when you have been neck-and-neck with the winner, the results allow you to measure the distance between what you thought was the best and what the jury did. Often you can outright disagree with the jury and think they made their decision for political reasons

Competition entry for Governors Island.

Diagram of recreation areas.

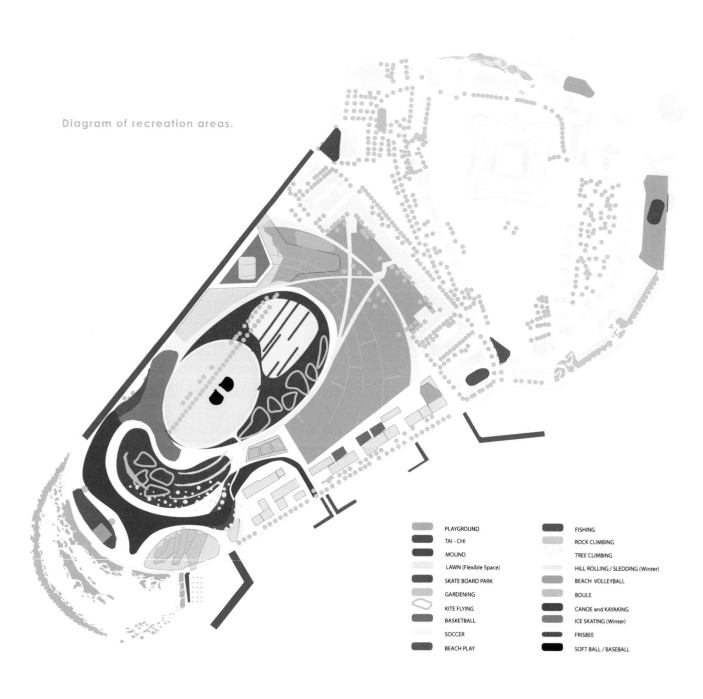

PLAYGROUND

TAI - CHI

MOUND

LAWN (Flexible Space)

SKATE BOARD PARK

GARDENING

KITE FLYING

BASKETBALL

SOCCER

BEACH PLAY

FISHING

ROCK CLIMBING

TREE CLIMBING

HILL ROLLING / SLEDDING (Winter)

BEACH VOLLEYBALL

BOULE

CANOE and KAYAKING

ICE SKATING (Winter)

FRISBEE

SOFT BALL / BASEBALL

or because they were not educated about what landscape is. But most of the time there is a grain of truth in the jury's decision that, if you forget about being competitive and defensive, can tell you a little bit more about who you are, what the culture is, and where you need to go. For my team, the 2007 Governors Island competition was just such an experience.

The project to reclaim Governors Island, an island in New York Harbor that had been a military and then a Coast Guard base until recently, as public space depended on a vision of civic landscape as funded, supported, and implemented by private development.

This vision of regeneration, dependent on the dynamic between private development and public agencies, is almost pro forma when considering how to regenerate a site.

The competition attracted an international roster of landscape architects and architects. The island, a historic district of fort and military campus to the north and a nondescript campus of buildings that were to be demolished to the south, was only a 5-minute boat ride from Lower Manhattan, with breathtaking views out to the harbor, the Verrazano Bridge, and the sparkling lights of the financial district. It was already a staggering experience to take the ferry and step onto the island. Once the doors opened, after the Coast Guard left, people would be able to get away from the city to an island in the city. But as it stood, people would arrive, check out the historic site, take in the spectacular views, and then leave. My team decided to make the place more accessible, more varied, with many programs for winter, spring, summer, fall, and for day and night, weekday and weekend. In physical layout, the plan channeled people to the different parts of the island. The plan also leveraged new development over 20 acres of the island to create and maintain 80 acres of new parkland. This arrangement has become the norm for public parks at least in the United States, as government money for building and maintaining public parks has dried up over the past few decades. Such partnerships are regenerative because they envision a time when the new development will provide not only the funding but also a critical category of users, the people who will take a proprietary interest in the new parkland.

Regeneration assumes that there will be some activity, whether it is the growth of a new forest or the flow of people to and from a new park, that will become the life of the place. We saw the opportunity at Governor's Island to create a place where there was a mutual benefit to all the component parts; they would build on each other.

Our team devised a nested landscape of places and activities that would extend people's visits from a couple hours, to a day, to a couple of weeks. In addition, we proposed that the new development—low-rise buildings for startups, light industry, and artisans—have green roofs that could extend the amount of park space right over new buildings.

The planning in the proposal took as much of our focus and concentration as the physical design. Our work is often not visible as design; it often requires an ability to lace together threads of different systems, from program to water systems to development criteria to street standards. When we propose a field of strawberries for city kids to be able to come in the summer and pick their own, it doesn't look like much. But in fact leveraging developers to cede their second floors to extend parkland over new buildings, identifying restaurant owners and spa operators who will buy in, and changing zoning, if need be, to accept a new vision of how people use a landscape and neighborhood, all these actions take tremendous care and thought and ingenuity.

Creating Places Where People Can Grow Food

So in our approach to Governors Island, people would be able to go out to Governors Island and not only take in the views but see a working farm and even participate in the farming. The draw of the landscape at exclusive vacation areas such as the Hamptons would be opened up to people who couldn't necessarily leave the city. The design of farmland within a public space requires a public–private partnership that blurs the boundary between public space and private enterprise and can entail a complex legal and management structure. But it also ensures that people will be able to engage in a different kind of activity that promotes health on many different levels. If one of Olmsted's goals was to create a green lung for the city that would

Farms on green roofs built over new development, increasing park space by 25 percent.

provide fresh air and a social space where people would learn to comport themselves, the goal of the twenty-first-century park is to reinterpret the methods, to integrate more active recreational, social, and commercial uses into the more passive nineteenth-century pastoral model of parkland.

Leveraging Developers to Build Parks and Topography

At Governors Island the demolition of the many undistinguished buildings on the totally flat landfill to the south would create an impressive amount of rubble. The materials, used as fill, could create a more varied topography. The first impulse in planning Governors Island oriented everyone to the spectacular views. But we also wanted to make places that actually relieved you of the sublime view. This varies the experience, and also, by orienting you to an interior space, heightens the impact of the amazing views when you go back out into the open. So there was an experiential aspect in conceiving of a new topography. Programmatically, we also wanted a place where kids could camp out and people could get into the water. The winds on Governors Island can be fierce, and the tidal currents around the island are treacherous. We wanted to create a sheltered place where people could engage in an entirely different experience of the landscape, not to mention getting into a kayak or canoe without risking their lives. But filling and sculpting a new series of hills that would cradle a kind of ravine landscape would be costly. Our proposal included the idea of creating requests for proposals for developers that would require them to build up the topography, so a resort developer such as Aman would submit a proposal not just for a new building but for a whole new landscape that would help to create new public space. The plan was an interconnected series of moves that would catalyze the private realm to generate public space and would allow the island to grow and change over time. The exercise proposed a dynamic planning structure that would ensure the health and responsible growth of the place over many years.

The winning scheme, by West8 and a team of local architects and landscape architects, looked nothing like our scheme. But the planning structure was remarkably similar: a phased plan that would result in a dynamic place where public and private operate together. Landscape designers and planners not only sculpt space but, maybe more importantly, propose and fashion social and economic structures that can perpetuate the public realm.

New topography creates a ravine for safe kayaking, camping, and a new spa built into the hill.

We knew, however much we were falling in love with our scheme, that we were missing the big move, the high-impact image, that would win the competition. It just never materialized. We won the Trenton waterfront redevelopment competition partly on the image of the garden bridges. Our Governors Island scheme was ingenious, with all the parts interconnected, a regeneration scheme that seemed to us foolproof. But smart systems do not win competitions. The lesson here was that we are by nature a group of designers who dive deep into a project and figure out a lot of the problems; we also can create iconic landscapes such as the Urban Garden Room (see p. 201). But at this stage of my career I couldn't necessarily do both at the same time.

Creating Habitat and Human Access Together

Proposal for a Great Lakes Park

When cities want to develop new parkland before the developer picture has become clear, a different strategy may be necessary. For a proposal for a park on one of the Great Lakes, we had to take into account the fact that the city

Lake Ontario island landfill.

is unlikely to be able to build the park in one phase. We developed the idea of a series of crater-like depressions. They could accommodate traditional park uses or could be designed to evolve as wildlife habitat; both approaches attract many park users. These were the only two we visualized in drawings; there are many other possibilities for such a modular system.

The crater approach would create new fill, which could be used to construct dunes on the pancake-flat landfill site, not only enhancing the site topographically but providing shelter from the harsh winds off the lake. So the crater concept creates new program at the same time that it creates new microclimate. It also accounts for changes in culture. For many decades, developers and planners tended to think that one use, a golf course, was most likely to generate value, whether by attracting buyers in private developments or income in public parks. Who knows what will be most useful, or marketable, a decade from now? A modular, incremental approach would allow the transformation of the flat landfill site to occur slowly, as resources became available. Then if at some time in the future a large effort gets the green light and the funding is available to make a more comprehensive and varied plan, the craters will be part of the whole, smaller spaces supporting a larger network. And if the money completely dries up after only a few have been made, then at least there will be something there. In projects where a derelict or inhospitable site can be transformed into something welcoming, but the resources are not there to take the route of complete reinvention, making these small moves, particularly if they are repetitive and so do not

Crater approach: wildlife sanctuary.

require a tremendous amount of design energy and money, can be like planting the seeds for something that will grow over many years.

To create a pedestrian path through the windswept site that also offers diversity for wildlife, we envisioned a bird wall that would be planted with vines and plants that otherwise do not grow on the flat, open topography. The bird wall also creates shelter from the wind for people walking, cycling, or jogging. An insertion like this to create a way of moving through the site can exist on its own, as a lone line through the landscape, or eventually become the spine of a more varied and articulated park.

Crater approach: traditional park.

LIBERTY STATE PARK, JERSEY CITY, NEW JERSEY

For Liberty State Park, we designed bird blinds that become little living walls as they grow. Even the architectural interventions can regenerate habitat.

The master plan for Liberty State Park offered a more comprehensive scheme of recreating wetland systems on the site. The restoration of a saltwater and a freshwater wetland would create a large amount of fill, which could then be used to create a more varied topography on the one corner of the site where a new recreational park was sited. The reason this project can be seen more as a regeneration project than restoration is that the process of succession from landfill to meadow and peat mats to woodland was already set in place over the past 40 years, since the rail lines that used to fill the site were decommissioned. The new wetlands were designed and implemented as isolated projects by the US Army Corps of Engineers; once they were constructed and the new park created from their fill, the site would be left alone to continue the process of reforestation, as pioneer species such as birch and aspens succeeded and the conditions are improved for more enduring species to grow. The plan was to monitor the new growth of seedlings and assembly of new communities over many years, to document the process of regeneration.

This kind of regeneration of wildlife habitat has become more commonly understood as a feature to be foregrounded. The interior of the park, which has been fenced off for years because of contamination left over from its years as a rail yard, had already become a favorite spot for birders and ecology enthusiasts. This new plan formalized the identity of Liberty State Park as a sanctuary. The regeneration of the site also included partial remediation of the site contamination as the new plants, some planted but most occurring naturally, colonized the interior and pulled contaminants out of the soils. But some of the contaminants, chromium in particular, do not respond to phytoremediation and have to be removed from the site to a depth of 4 feet or more and possibly capped before they are replaced with clean fill and topsoil. The plan needed to respond to these contingencies: What if certain areas could never be cleaned up? How do you limit access? A series of movable boardwalks would allow the circulation to be flexible, moving wherever it was found that it was safe to go.

The regeneration of Liberty State Park was not only ecological; as the park went from hazardous landfill to forest, meadow, and wetland, the surrounding neighborhoods, the old upland community of Jersey City as

The interior successional landscape is a mosaic of woodlands, wetlands, meadows, and bog mats, with a new park, created from material excavated for the new wetlands, in the foreground.

well as new waterfront developments along the harbor, would begin to see the park as an amenity and not a wasteland. Property values would rise as the park was recast as recreational open space. By the twenty-first century, new developments had begun to showcase wildlife preserves, or conservation areas, as selling points. The emerald green of golf courses, maintained by a constant stream of fertilizer and herbicides and pesticides, has been supplanted in some cases by the changing colors of meadows and forests. The wildlife sanctuary is becoming the golf course of the twenty-first century. Planners and designers can no longer think that parkland will perpetuate itself because a city or government thinks it is good. The conception of new parkland more often than not in this era depends on an economic or social structure that will allow the landscape to regenerate over many years.

New park plan.

Chapter 6:

Expression

We return to the question that began this book: Are we engaging in art or ecology? Up to this point this book has focused on strategies and systems—natural, social, cultural—at work in making change to the landscape. In many cases aesthetic operations such as a choice of material have served a larger goal, such as making connections between things that have been cut off or distanced from each other. The explicit goal is to make things better, or do a good job, or serve a community or a client.

A goal that often flies under our professional radar is the desire to make something, to express something, to deploy our creative powers in the service of beauty, or a certain emotional power that is hard to articulate. Most of the projects I have ever worked on have this aspect to them. It is difficult to describe, impossible to quantify, but our projects would fall down without it and just be serviceable.

Once we have integrated green practices into our very fiber, we need to ask ourselves, "How do we approach design?" Do we really start with the systems and overlays, à la McHarg, or the Leadership in Energy and Environmental Design checklists, or the desire to do what our friends and colleagues are doing? Many of us still tap into the formal agenda that we have always nurtured and tested throughout our lives; the agenda leads us to make beautiful places, to be interested in seeing what will happen if we set up a rigid and visibly artificial geometry against the flux of natural processes. Or sometimes our agenda is simply to express something that the place, or the team, or the problem statement evoked in us.

I would prefer to steer clear of a discussion of what beauty is, except to say that what interests me is not how perfect something can be formally but the oddness that occurs naturally when you are trying to serve more than one agenda, or just when you encounter something unexpected, and the resolution that allows these agendas to coexist comfortably. This appreciation of things that do not follow a formula, that have something intrinsically different about them, tends not to subscribe to the belief that beauty occurs when everything is perfect and nothing left out. I prefer the description of beauty in Edgar Allen Poe's 1838 story "Ligeia": "There is no exquisite beauty . . . without some strangeness in the proportion."

Many of us came to the field of landscape design through the art route, and even those who came to it from ecology often have a hidden or unexplored proclivity for making things because they are just arresting or beautiful or formally interesting. The ecologists I know have a deep appreciation of the aesthetic value of the landscape and usually an attachment to particular landscapes that goes well beyond science. If art is an expression of the creative imagination, and if the artifact is valued for its aesthetic qualities or emotional power, works of landscape design, and also many works of ecological restoration, can be considered art more often than not.

Peter Walker did teach me to focus on one thing at a time, and I would like to follow his direction for the final projects in this book. Each project is presented as an expression of one idea or feeling. I do this not just to demonstrate the artistic impulse behind each work but so that the reader will ask for herself or himself on each project, "What is the one thing I am trying to express here?" It helps immeasurably in holding on to the art part as you ride the bumpy ride of ecology, community, and all the other aspects of environmental design. In the end, we are making something.

Expressing a Culture or Cultures

The Boxwood Farm, Oldwick, New Jersey

In formalized gardens as well as wild ones, people can experience the dynamism of the landscape, whether it's the experience of growth over time or of processing through a space. At this private farm, a boxwood farm in western New Jersey, what could have been designed as a standard nursery grid was manipulated to provide a variety of vantage points and places to pause and rest. These photos are of year 1 after planting and year 8. Here, over the 20 years I have worked on this project with the client, the question to me has been, "How is the farm a garden and the garden a farm?" The resulting landscape is an expression of what a farm is: The Boxwood Farm is a highly formalized place that brings the operations of laying out fields and utility, maintaining a living landscape, into relief.

I was called onto this project in 1993, when the client had commissioned Steven Harris to turn a small house with cottage into a farm compound. The client asked me what she could plant in an adjoining field that could be sold commercially, and because the abundant deer population tromps through the reforested old stone farm pens, the only thing I could think of was boxwood, one of the few plants that deer won't destroy. The layout of the field—about 2,000 baby Korean boxwoods of three varieties—took on a life of its own as I started to lay it out as a strolling garden for the client. What could have been a pragmatic exercise became an expressive one, with the overlaid grids of boxwood, clipped yearly, becoming something to explore. The client has a wickedly keen eye and occupies the overlapping territories of fashion and art. The boxwood farm became an exploration of the intersection of agriculture and art, a confluence that reaches back millennia, through certain French garden traditions all the way to the earliest representations of the Garden of Eden.

Even in the more garden-like spaces, the idea of cultivation, and of plants as specimens, is legible.

Boxwood Farm right after planting.

Boxwood Farm, year 5.

DRAWING ON TRADITION

The Boxwood Farm drew on the different traditions of landscape management: agricultural, gardening, and native forest. But it recast them in a way that is abstracted from or removed from the original. It took its cues from the orderly disposition of human artifacts: the nursery, the lawn, the herb

Corn crib pool house
by Steven Harris Architects.

Revamped cottage garden,
now sculpture garden.

garden, the water garden. The design for the boxwood fields themselves grew out of overlapping, canted rectilinear grids, a very simple geometry of three overlays. All of these moves required that we know the original, know the rules that govern a cottage garden (the mosaic of textures, for example) or a farm field (the widths between rows necessary for maintenance).

Then we overlaid our own rules, which were defined over the course of working with the client and the site. The cottage garden had to have no more than five plant species, because the client has a quite minimalist sensibility; the grids of the boxwood field had to cross at a central point, where we sited the stone terrace; and the three different orientations of the grid had to be legible only from the client's dressing room window.

Water garden at the edge
of the boxwood fields.

The client's vanity, the one place from which the overlay of the grids is legible.

In every project that is in the realm of expression, we somehow divine a set of rules that we follow as they interact with the materiality of the site. The resulting landscape is never the same from one project to the next, even when the site and program are the same. The introduction of a new client, and the passing of time and experience of other projects, make repetition impossible. The Boxwood Farm is a product of a particular time: the early 1990s, when the vernacular landscape was a favorite subject for architects and landscape designers alike. It may now seem conventional. But when it was built, it integrated this vernacular predilection with a formal rigor that normally was reserved for gardens, not farms. The patterns of work and growth are clearly legible throughout.

READING THE PATTERNS OF LIFE

Two decades later, our work had been transformed by the popularization of the concept of fractals—the class of shapes in geometry in which the whole is split into parts that reflect the shape of the whole, in min-

Terrace within the boxwood field.

iature—and by computer technology that can generate such shapes. Before this time, at least as far as we know, Western landscape traditions had tended to contrast "geometric" form against "organic" or "natural" form—that is, grids and circles and triangles, the stuff of fourth-grade geometry, the backbone of the royal French landscape, held in opposition to seemingly hand-drawn, or nature-made, curvilinear forms, such as the serpentine in London's Hyde Park. With the advent of fractals, we started to see natural form as intensely geometric, finally recognizing the rigorous geometry that produces snowflakes, ferns, waterways, and crystals, among other forms. The composition of fractals shows the infinite recursion of the pattern of the whole into the pattern of the tiniest detail. Fractals, catching on in the late 1990s in landscape and architecture schools, really appealed to those of us reared in the psychedelic haze of the 1960s. In fractal geometry, everything is connected, and everything is exquisitely beautiful, as you can see in the image blow.

Coney Island in its heyday.

Forms of marine life; forms of Coney Island structures.

The wall along the boardwalk presents a bunker-like face to the city.

New York Aquarium, Coney Island, New York

When I was invited to compete for the design of a new perimeter for the New York Aquarium in Coney Island, in 2006, my team and I were stunned by the beauty of the exhibits—jellyfish, octopus, corals, sharks—and the formal patterning was comprehensible to us in terms of the beauty of infinite recursion. We were asked to design a treatment for the perimeter that would transform the aquarium from a bunker-like aggregation of exhibits into something cohesive, something that would announce the aquarium's presence to the city and identify the aquarium as a part of Coney Island. The solution, we felt, needed to grow out of the infinitely exquisite forms of sea life revealed in the aquarium's exhibits.

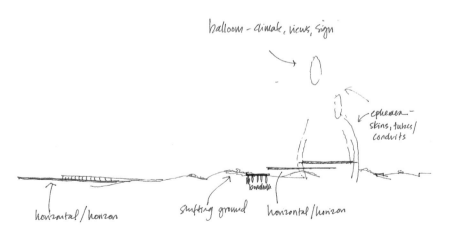

The author's initial diagrams.

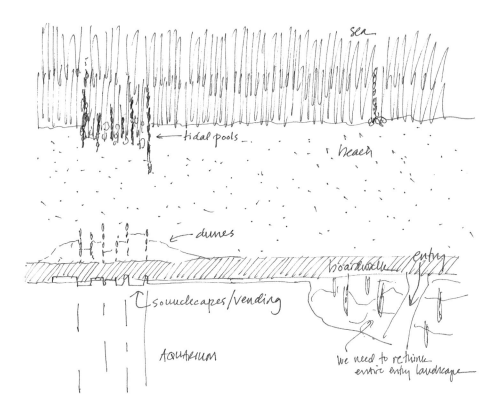

I invited two architects to work with me on the competition. I drew the diagram at top at our first working session: a light structure that raised up above the aquarium and the beach and the street, creating a new member in the family of constructions that have given Coney Island its identity, such as the Cyclone and the Parachute Jump.

I knew that we needed to rethink the perimeter on the ground. I invited two Austrian architects, Peter Ebner and Franziska Ullmann, to design the earth-based structures at the ground. But I knew we needed light, since Coney Island is all about light, so I invited Barcelona architect Enric Ruiz-Geli of Cloud 9, known for his scrims, or skins, of LEDs, to design an ephemeral structure of light.

The design brings the exhibits of the aquarium out to the beach and the city. A newly constructed dune landscape demonstrates dune ecology; a new tidal habitat would be built in between the existing groins at the beach. I identified a marine biologist with the Army Corps of Engineers who is experimenting with creating new ephemeral habitats in just such a condition, new tidal pools constructed on the beach between existing groins, or jetties.

The landscape plan extends
the aquarium out to the sea.

EXPRESSING NATURAL FORCES

The skin of the new perimeter would interact with the sun: 40,000 solar-powered LEDs would glow different colors according to how much sun they received each day, from blue at the highest solar exposure to red at the lowest. Water would also flow through the skins, filtering the aquarium's water. The skins work as the aquarium's gills. We studied the similarities between how fish skin works and how architectural surfaces work.

The model looking into the
aquarium, under the web.

The new structure resembles a whale shark; the resemblance was not originally intentional but grew out of the function of opening out to the city.

Ceramic tiles designed by Cloud 9 act like a shark's skin to deflect water.

The landscape plan shows how the perimeter, far from acting as a boundary for the aquarium, creates a porous membrane through which the aquarium's programs flow in and out.

The model gives a sense of the energy of the design, pulling together the disparate buildings of the aquarium under one overarching open structure. The team consulted with Frei Otto, the master of tensile structures, about the web. His enthusiastic summary and endorsement: "It's sculpture."

The web structure consists of a series of arches and masts, holding up the mesh. The masts splay out at the top to support ethylene tetrafluoroethylene roofs, which could provide shelter in the winter. The perimeter concept also addresses the harsh winter conditions at Coney Island, which faces the open Atlantic Ocean.

The model for the perimeter, which in Ruiz-Geli's workshop became a whole overarching structure, was made by a Barcelona dress designer. I show these images not because I can claim authorship of the web, as it came to be called, but to show the result of the working sessions in which I brought these designers together to collaborate with me on a project that needed to regenerate not only the aquarium but Coney Island itself. The formal solution is such a statement, an expression of marine life but also a magnificent form in itself. Regeneration was a major goal of the project; a solution that was closer to art than architecture or landscape design had the power to transform the site into something sublime.

Creating a New Urban Ecology

If you were following the purely programmatic (design a new edge) or the ecological (create a new marine ecology for the aquarium), you would not necessarily end up with a glowing, blinking structure to add to the family of structures (the Cyclone, the Parachute Jump) at Coney Island. The evocative poetry of Cloud 9's web speaks to people's deepest connections, with a beloved place, with wonder, with life. It operates at the intersection of science

and infrastructure, ecology and art. But ultimately it resonates as an artistic response to the question of how to reinvent the aquarium to be more transparent and to connect to the other structures on Coney Island.

As a landscape designer, I knew that landscape alone would not transform the aquarium. Cloud 9 responded with a fantastical whale shark. Although you can see the intention of my original diagrams, you can also see how it took on a life of its own. This is often what designers hope for when we bring people in to collaborate with us.

The Urban Garden Room, One Bryant Park, New York City

There were several reasons that we approached the Urban Garden Room as an art project. My team and I were asked to design a green sculpture for the winter garden at One Bryant Park. Although one response would be to make a minimalist array of green walls—a living architecture within the modern architecture of the building—we also responded to a previous version of a sculpture for the space, designed by the building's architects, Cook + Fox, that you could walk under. There are a number of rules implicit in the brief and our response. We were asked to make something that felt "natural" (rule 1), but the tall, skinny space of the winter garden did not seem to accommodate any sort of faux nature, something that mimics an actual landscape, without seeming kitschy. Also, because of the limited sun, it couldn't support trees and shrubs very well (rule 2); they would have grown diagonally up toward the east, where most of the available sunlight came from. So we had a problem: How were we to make something "natural" in such an artificial, vertical space?

Often when I am faced with a problem that seems so difficult, I try to think of an analogy or precedent. What is a landscape out in nature that is tall, vertical, and makes you feel enveloped in a natural environment? We thought of the fern canyons of northern California, and the image below generated the ideas for the Urban Garden Room.

Inspired by the fern canyons of Humboldt County, California.

EXPRESSING EARTH

We were intrigued by the idea that we could make something that you could actually enter, and we thought of making a vertical environment, a living sculpture, covered with ferns, cresses, and other plants. We also thought we needed to work with a sculptor, because we were treading into a territory of sculptural form at a scale that was completely new to us (checklist item: know when to pull in the professionals). The project was on such a fast track that we couldn't delay the process by interviewing artists, getting fee proposals, and then starting the design process from scratch, so we asked the nearest sculptor who could jump into the project. That was my mother, Dorothy Ruddick, a Bauhaus-trained painter and sculptor who had been enlarging her small maquettes of human figures into large bronze sculptures for the past several years. She was game, and she accepted the challenge.

We did some studies of arches. The work needed to be somewhat evocative of a natural bridge or archway but clearly manmade. The result is an expression of a natural form that in no way looks like nature writ small or stuffed into a small urban space. When people walk into the space they feel the cooling effects of the plants and the earth out of which they are growing, but the forms also engage their imaginations. The place will be memorable for them not because of how responsible or green it is but because of the way it makes them feel. It is green, but it is also delightful.

CREATING A LIVING LANDSCAPE

Dorothy Ruddick wasn't the only artist involved in the project. Many of the people on the team, including the designers from WRT, including me, had art backgrounds. The fabricators, Mosaiculture Internationale de Montreal, is headed by a landscape architect. The metal fabricator brought as much art as technology to his forming of the structures; the plantsman, who took the sketches we did and interpreted them with plants, is an artist. It takes more than technicians to create a great landscape; it takes artists as well. So while juggling the checklists and operations that will make you feel as if you are helping the planet, your fellow humans, and your own family, don't forget one

of the most important items on anyone's checklist, which is to have fun, to savor the joy we get in making the things we can make together.

The Mosaiculture Internationale team constructed the four sculptural objects in thirteen pieces, planted them in their greenhouses in Lavalle, Quebec, and then shipped them down to be assembled on the site. The finished sculptures stand from 6 feet to 25 feet tall. The structures are composed of a metal skeleton; a wire mesh cladding, or skin; and a geotextile fabric wrapping the mesh. The fabric-wrapped mesh skin was then packed with a light soil mixture and laced with irrigation lines. The plants were then planted in holes in the fabric. After 3 months of growth, the plants had grown together, and the sculptures were ready to go. On September 12, 2009, the sculptures were trucked in pieces from Quebec to New York City, where they were assembled over the course of 2 days and nights.

People are always in the Urban Garden Room, from opening to closing. It feels cool and moist, and the air feels cleaner. The Urban Garden Room is an expression of an idea about a green canyon. The signature green space for the city's ultimate green building is not about performance; at this scale that would be pointless. It is about what it feels like to be in nature while not looking like a copy or miniaturized version of a "natural" landscape. The odd shapes—the points on the archway, the torque in one of its legs—took it out of the realm of realistic representation. It is a reinterpretation of a landscape that exists on the other side of the country.

EXPRESSING TOPOGRAPHY

Kinderhook Retreat, Kinderhook, New York

When I met Steven Harris and Lucien Rees Roberts in 1992, they had built a studio for Rees Roberts and a house for them and their guests in upstate New York. It was narrow and tall: about 13 feet wide, 35 feet long, and 25 feet high, with a basement bedroom. The building—a shingled box, really—sat at the top of a hill on the property, which sits at one of the highest points in Columbia County. We know this because Rees Roberts found the land by poring over US Geological Survey topographic maps, looking for high points.

The building's siting at the top of the hill was both dramatic and problematic. The 360-degree views from the house took in Hunter Mountain and the Catskills across the Hudson River. The austerity of the small but tall box atop the hill was striking. But there was not much of a foreground to all the views, and the austerity could become a little too austere in the dead of winter. Part of the problem was that the drive, which was built as the construction access, rammed straight up the hill, and you screeched to a halt in front of the building.

It was a little mean, and it felt as if you were being dropped off at the peak of a mountain and would have to be helicoptered out if anything went seriously wrong.

The landscape of Columbia County had appealed to Harris and Rees Roberts because it is farmland with wide open spaces and a softly rolling topography. There was nothing sweet or manufactured about the place; it was a working landscape with some of the most spectacular views in the Hudson River Valley. Harris sometimes uses the word *tough* to describe a design; it is the ultimate compliment from him. But their collaborative work also has a lyrical quality to it, and a painterly quality; Rees Roberts is a landscape painter as well as an architect. The Columbia County landscape is both tough and lyrical.

We all knew that the entry drive had to be redesigned. Harris organized for the best bulldozer operator in the state to meet us on-site for 2 days, and we regraded the whole approach to bring the drive around the hill, to a parking area well below the elevation of the house. We spent the 2 days walking in front of the master operator, sculpting the topography with him to create a curving drive that allowed the water to flow under it at one point.

Grading is an art form. It is an art form in design but also in execution. This particular machine operator is in high demand because he does something with the earth that is very subtle, too subtle to document on a drawing. When he has finished sculpting the earth there is a little "lift" to the topography that makes the transition between virgin soils and newly disturbed earth seamless. It is as if he has tapped into the soft curvatures of the earth. This level of artistry is something innate; either you have it or you don't. We try to engage operators like this on all of our projects that require regrading. If you happen to work with someone who doesn't have it, the landforms look more engineered, almost like landfill. No matter how much you point and explain, it always looks manufactured. There are some projects where this is a desired look, but those have to be conceived as art as well, taking topography into the realm of pure sculpture. But on these residential projects where the goal is to feel connected to the larger landscape the "lift" effect is a requirement. Once we were done, the straight ramp to the house was gone, and a new, curving drive nestled into a graciously rolling topography.

For years friends asked Harris and Rees Roberts when they were going to make "the big house," and several generations of designs experimented with three-story volumes, towers, and other figures that would make the studio almost into an outbuilding. After more than 15 years, Harris finally came up with a strategy for the "big house": He designed the living space—a kitchen and dining space, two bedrooms, and two bathrooms—to fit into the exact same envelope as the studio and turned it 90 degrees so that this new "box" was perpendicular to the old "box." He had his own agenda, including referring for this most luxurious vacation home to the exact dimensions of a common trailer, the kind he would have seen in his own neighborhood growing up in Jacksonville, Florida. And it is a luxurious, not to say sublime space, using such economy of means in terms of dimensions. He also could have been pushing back at the culture we live in, and where many of our clients have come from, in which more space equals better. It's a luxurious space in less than 1,000 square feet.

The architects/owners built this wall as one of their first moves, to define a flat space for "the perfect lawn."

Croquet on "the perfect lawn."

The steps up to the house carved into the topography.

The meadow seems to slide right through the dining room, which slides open on both sides.

This gutsy move, constraining oneself with an almost ridiculous set of spatial rules to make something exquisite and generous, did something interesting to the site. Whereas before the box sat kind of dumbly on top of a hill, now the two buildings made a space between, a domestic space, and stretched out into the landscape. Adding one identical volume created a landscape, and the topography within which the two were set came to the foreground.

By this point my former student and by then colleague David Kelly had begun working with Harris and Rees Roberts in their office on their landscapes, as the large urban projects I was working on were taking up all my time, plus the interconnectedness of architecture and landscape made an in-house landscape designer a great asset. Kelly took the lead on this next phase of the landscape, paving the terrace between the two buildings with permeable pavers, planting them with thyme, and adding an orchard to the slope down to the driveway. His work didn't stop there; eventually he designed and had built a firepit and a spring-fed pond at the bottom of the woodland.

Every part of this project is about the shaping of the earth, its texture, sun and shadow. The rigor of the buildings suggested a rigor of landscape where nothing is extra. What is expressed is not just the topography but something of the spareness and economy of the Upstate landscape. The design expresses something of the culture of the region: economy of means when people have little, but also self-restraint when people are given much.

Biscayne Bay Garden, Miami Beach, Florida

I have collaborated with architect Dennis Wedlick and Barlis Wedlick Architects for more than 20 years. When a repeat client asked us to rethink the landscape of a villa overlooking Biscayne Bay in Miami Beach, our collaboration took on a new cast, as we worked together as one office to redesign the landscape. The seams between outside and inside are often blurry, but in this case they were almost nonexistent, so operating as one helped knit the work together, just as Kelly has done with Harris and Rees Roberts.

The existing house sat lengthwise across the site, separating the long approach drive and forecourt from a back yard with a pool sitting slightly above the water level of the bay. The program was loose, with a pool and

places to sit the only requirements. Looking out at the back—the foreground of lawn and pool and bridge, the middle ground a vast expanse of water, and the background the skyline of Miami—I had a thought I have had many times in my career. The presence of the bay was so powerful, amplified by

the distant cityscape, that I thought, "Anything we do here is going to seem ridiculous unless it is really big." A garden that is about itself is going to be dwarfed by the views. The traditional concept of a garden, that it is somehow bounded, looking back to the roots of the word in the Old German word for "enclosure," is challenged by many of the project briefs we receive. In a bustling cityscape such as Queens Plaza, you had to take the infrastructure into the space considered the project, because it was so imposing that trying to create something that did not take it into its boundaries would fail; a foregrounded landscape that did not embrace the "background" of the infrastructure would seem weak.

Spa area
of pool.

Dense "jungle"
walk to water.

Similarly at this Biscayne Bay project, any design that didn't take in the water and city would seem dinky. We tried to make an elegant garden of stone and water, inspired by the Museum of Modern Art garden designed originally by Philip Johnson. But everything we tried looked inconsequential when viewed against the water. A trip to the Miami Beach Botanical Garden triggered an idea for Dennis and me: A large pond creates a sense of scale far greater than the rest of the garden, and the water acts as a foil to the wild plantings of palms and other tropicals. What if the whole back yard were water? So we started to draw the landscape as a series of planes, the largest of which would be the bay itself. You would walk through intense gardens on either side to get out to the water and the views, your horizon line punctuated by the spires of Miami Beach.

You walk through a jungly garden to one side, or a more domesticated but lush ginger garden with palms to the other side, to get out to the water.

Once you are out there you see the faceted landscape of pool and spa resting on a water garden sitting over the bay. The language of the landscape is an extension of the house, although there is something tighter and more modern about the landscape, intentionally.

Ginger garden with palms.

Coral found on-site was crushed
to fill the sausage tree pit.

Bridge between ginger garden,
right, and fern island, left.

The water was moved right back to the building's colonnade.

BEING WITH WATER

The living space extends out over the water garden, nestled into plantings on three sides but opening out to the water.

Snakeplant, considered a cliché in a dentist's office or a pest in a native tropical landscape, here is showcased for its sculptural form.

A kind of bridge landscape of native leatherleaf ferns and exotic alocasias brings you out to the floating platform.

The fern island, inspired by Florida's native tussocks, also contains alocacia, an exotic.

Fatsia and
native ferns.

From every angle you see the new landscape in relation to the water of the
bay and the city beyond.

From some angles the water garden and pool are only minimally distinguished from the larger waterbody. Architect and landscape designer worked closely together on all the dimensions of the landscape, both to relate to the building in scale and to connect with the water.

We discovered something about what we thought would be a garden that was all about water. It is actually as much about the sky. The reflections change by the minute, and no two minutes are ever the same. So the garden not only launches you into the wider, wilder water of the bay, it actually raises you up to feel as if you can almost touch the sky. The forms and patterns of clouds and the constantly changing color and quality of the sky become the subject of this garden.

As with any art, landscape design can take you in directions you cannot anticipate. Setting up a basic premise—the governing idea of what this place is about—and giving yourself some stringent rules and guidelines, you can discover that you have traveled to a place you could not have imagined. This is the thrill of gardens, or parks and streetscapes and all of our built environments: that they can resituate us in relation to the natural world and restore connections we may have forgotten were there.

Something interesting happened when we did all this water on the bay side of the site. The client unexpectedly purchased a major work of environmental art, the *Lunar Lander* by Spencer Finch, and decided that the place to site it would be at the front drive, right in front of the house. Ideally, our clients are our collaborators, with input that pushes us in directions we may not have gone in. Once we had completed the waterfront garden, and it was quite dramatic and unexpected, our client felt that the front was almost a ruse, a drive that brought you through a landscape of royal palms and into the house through a lush forecourt.

The front had been almost a neutral foil to the back; the sculpture turned the front landscape into a neutral foil for this oddly beautiful object. With the addition of the *Lunar Lander*, we had to rethink the front to accept such a big work—big in concept, in presence, in addition to scale. So we brought in huge Bismarck palms, fatter than the royals and silver-hued, and sited them around the drive. The new plantings brought the *Lunar Lander* down in scale so it would feel as if it had landed in a front garden without blowing it out of scale. We also enhanced the allée of palms at the drive, so now the long drive of royal palms ends at a glowing orb tinted to be the exact color of the moon as it appears in this area of Florida.

Spencer Finch's
Lunar Lander.

SEEING WHERE IT TAKES YOU

With the addition of this new object in the front, the water garden becomes less of a one-liner, not the only arresting moment but one part of a whole that has, in its conception, a certain oddness that makes it mysterious and beautiful. Projects like this are exciting and fun; we transformed the rather pedestrian back yard into a dream landscape. And once we did that the client felt that the front landscape needed something different and maybe startling. One move leads to another, through the structure of the rules you have set up.

We thought the bayfront garden was about water, but it brings the sky right down to Earth. We thought the front was a kind of neutral setup for the drama of the water in the bayside garden. But in fact the front became a dramatic entry sequence with the addition of a somewhat mesmerizing object. And the fact that the glowing object seems to have alighted from the sky reinforces that sense that this landscape is as much about sky as it is about water.

What Are We Doing Here, Anyway?

An underlying message of this book is that people can feel deeply connected to wild landscapes. I hope people will own them—feel that they are part of them, that they are responsible for the care of their landscapes, that they understand when they should just leave their places alone, when they need to manage them, when they need to transform them. I hope people will perceive the landscape as alive. This seems more important than ever now that the planet is facing climate change and mass extinctions. Ultimately we are banking on a future in the landscape for our children.

There was a period of time in my life, in the 1990s and later, when the most high-profile landscape designers considered it outside their scope to plan for the kinds of things children want to do in parks and gardens. Playground design fell to specialists in ordering furnishings, not designers. But the era of sustainability has shifted the focus back to children, not only because the activities of children bring other people to public spaces but because whereas members of older generations have to rewire our brains to adopt environmentally conscious behaviors, children can be taught from birth how to recycle, how to conserve energy, how to manage places for wildlife. Also, the world belongs to them, or they belong to the world, in a way that will cascade down through future generations.

At the Living Water Park, children spend hours on activities like this, watching how water flows from one level to the next. Their fascination with natural processes translates into a natural sense of stewardship. When I was teaching a 1-week course at Schumacher College, a sustainable design program in Devon, England, several years ago, I gave a talk one evening illustrating the kinds of planning and design work I do. After the talk, several students, who ranged in profession from architect to nurse, asked me to talk about what sustainability means in their own daily lives, as opposed to in their work.

Promoting Stewardship

Looking through my laptop images I came across a video of my daughter learning to use push-pins on a family bulletin board—turning them the right way, pushing gently, learning by trial and error how not to prick her fingertips, and finally, when she had successfully pinned up a new school notice, saying, under her breath, "I did it." As I looked at this video, thinking about what I could tell my students who wanted to do better for the planet, I thought that if we ourselves learned to treat every living organism and nonliving component of our landscape with as much protectiveness as my daughter was exercising over her fingertips, we might be able to hardwire our brains to do less damage.

I know this rewiring works, through positive reinforcement and aversion therapy. Everyone wants rewards for doing well or doing good. And it's only natural to internalize the negative effects of certain behaviors: the fingers getting pricked, or the ever-rising landfills polluting our water, or greenhouse gases turning the heat up on our planet. This internalizing—or compassion for the world around us—can't help but lead to action. If our children can take into their own bodies the ability to feel when damage is being done—and the younger generations actually are doing this—we might actually be able to reverse some of the damage we as a species have done, or at least slow it down.

But then there is design. Of course, changing the way we think and the way we act could possibly help us survive, as a planet, but designers are also engaged in something more visceral than just addressing the wiring of our brains to develop the other-care gene. There is the sensuous aspect of what we do as well, the tactile, sensory level on which it is working. We get a lot of joy out of making and tending wild landscapes.

This wildflower meadow would have been lawn in another era. Now it is a wildlife refuge for birds and other animals, but also for the people who live here. It retains stormwater, slowing it down as it moves downhill, eventually toward the Hudson River, recharging the groundwater. We can check off the devices we used on a project (bioswales, detention basin) as a feature, rather than as an eyesore, in the development of wildlife sanctuary as parkland for the community. And in terms of economic development, this approach seizes on the stormwater management and wildlife sanctuary as the golf course of the twenty-first century, raising property values in the surrounding neighborhood. We can change the culture to make places that function more as ecologically whole systems economically appealing.

But in focusing our attention on environmental systems, we are also focusing on connections between people and places. And no matter how well you design a system, the most compelling factor in creating places that people will care for, tend, safeguard, and really live in is the way they feel and look, the way they function as places for living. So make bioswales, make pavement permeable, generate all of your energy off the grid, but ultimately make beautiful places for people to love.

Making Beautiful Places

The ability to design our environment is a gift. It is fun, engaging, sooth-ing, it brings people together, and it takes your mind off difficult issues and sometimes even helps you sort things out without your knowing it. It can be meditative. So in the age of ecological design we can't forget how transforma-tive design is, as a practice. It's not just about making the planet better. It often makes us feel better; it makes our lives work better.

In the scientific agenda of ecological design, we can't forget how great it feels just to make something beautiful, to dip our feet into cool water, to walk through a meadow. We can't forget that while we are making our worlds less carbon producing, more water conserving, while we are rethinking how our children are spending their time and what lessons we are teaching them, they also really love to run through a meadow.

We need to safeguard the things that give us joy. We can't forget that joy is part of design and a major part of life that is necessary for our survival. We love to design our environments because it's an activity that makes us happy, as well as a job, or a task that helps us feel that we are doing something good.

Remembering the Joy Part

We have to remember that the end product of all our work is pleasure in our surroundings, relief from stress, and connection to something bigger than ourselves. At the Living Water Park, when the water has been settled, aerated, and filtered, the lessons learned are undeniable: lessons about phytoremediation, the usefulness of wetlands, and the potential role of humans in perpetuating a healthful life cycle. But the end product of our work is also how great it feels for these Chengdu citizens to wade in cool water in a beautiful pool on a very hot summer day.

The projects I have done that are most successful are the projects that give the people who live there a lot of joy: getting a phone call from a client who has seen an oriole, or from a husband whose wife didn't like traveling to their weekend house but now spends weeks at a time there, or seeing children experiencing their first fireflies or looking for worms. It is the order, though, as well as the abundance of life that makes these places work. People feel as if they are a structural part of these landscapes because of the domesticated qualities of the design that make them home.

My own back yard landscape is a place of wonder for me, always changing, home to birds year-round, to crickets, but also to my barbecue and the big Komodo dragon sculpture. When I walk through it, or just sit in the back taking it in, it is not the volume of water the landscape is retaining or the amount of carbon sequestered by all those leaves that makes me happy. It is the color of pokeweed in the fall, the delicacy of asters, the fluffy milkweed seedpods.

Once you have shifted into the mindset that does not isolate what is wild from what is design, the beauty of each species seems as intentional as the most formal of gardens. Bringing these two scales together—the scale of the designed landscape and the scale of a single species—is our challenge for the next decades.

Acknowledgments

This book started with a question from Metropolis Books' Diana Murphy: "Do you have a book for us?" Well yes, I thought, I may just have a book in me, and so it started. Eventually we landed at Island Press, with the superb editor Courtney Lix. But it is fitting to acknowledge Diana Murphy: instigator, visioneer, adventurer, and pretty selfless birther of books.

Courtney Lix is actually a real old-style editor, from aerial view to tiny details. She knows how to build you up for a big push; and redirect you gently when things start to veer off course. She is a born diplomat, but also crystal-clear on what needs to happen, and an excellent writer as well.

The many people who have contributed with everything they have to the work in this book are listed here, according to our serial studios: the orange-floor loft: Judith Heintz, Diana Drake, Dale Russell, Susannah Drake; the attic: Samantha Harris and David Kelly; the basement: Greg Webster, Anna Forrester, Pallavi Nadkarni; the little office on Germantown: Jason Bregman, Devinder Soin, Abby Feldman, Andee Mazzocco, Patty Hume, Kim Soles, LaTonya Matthews, Jim Mullahy, Craig Pocock, Ilse Frank, Christine Graziano. Elizabeth Hammill, Chris Mendel, Dorrett Linton and her wild rides; the WRT tower: My Ly, Jen Orr, Hee Yeun Yoon—who with her family and my lifetime friend Alice Choy opened the door to Seoul for me—Jennifer Martell, Keiko Cramer, Misa Chen, Abdallah Tabet, Doug Meehan, Karen Blanchard; the coral-walled office: Judith Heintz (again), Diana Drake (again), Martha Burgess; Steven Yavanian, Josh Kent, Pippa Brashear, and John Beckman. Our virtual team 2009 through 2013: Adam Schatz, Ashley Young, Khoa Dam (my hero), Maggie Hansen, Eliza Shaw Valk. And always: David Kelly, who went from being my student to my employee to my protégé to my peer.

A thank you to the most recent configuration: Karl Krause, the first mastermind in the post-nomadic era; Murray Kamara, who is so skilled and also so game; my right hand Zoulikha Ben-Rahou; Kate Farquhar, and Kim Soles (again) who brings her nature spirits with her, and knows my habits and methods better than anyone.

This book reflects the hands and sensibilities and computer-graphic skills of many—Abby Feldman's startling color sense, Steven Yavanian's nuanced textures. It takes a particular sense of humor to tolerate my analog art direction, especially when it's in PowerPoint.

This book evolved in partnership with artist and graphic designer Lazslo Nosek, whose huge talents as well as conveniently later time zone helped us experiment with not one, not two, but maybe ten versions of this book.

From lectures to press to cocktail parties I never would have thought to co-host, communications guru Saverio Mancina has tapped into his Inner Canadian, helping to steward this wild thing not only with equanimity but enthusiasm, and patience. He navigates with grace both the ambitious vision and allergy to trendiness of our studio.

This book is witness to partnerships. Steven Harris and Lucien Rees-Roberts are geniuses, artists, and friends of a lifetime. They have provided substantial intellectual and professional support; their friendship; a yearly respite on the most magical island idyll, where several versions of this book were laid out. Our many projects bridging the architecture/landscape divide are documented in these pages by Scott Frances, the rare architectural photographer who makes landscapes feel in a photograph as rich and layered as they are in real life. Dennis Wedlick, really a landscape architect in architect's clothing, has given me opportunities and a unique collaborative friendship, but also invaluable perspective, explaining me to me with gems such as "Margie, I have learned over the years that you just need ... time." A thank you to all the therapist/priests in my life, formally trained or otherwise.

The list of friends and family who gave me invaluable support is long, really long, given how long this book was kicking around: the brutally honest, and brilliant, Susan Fine; Elizabeth Estabrook, who kept listening without complaint; Sally Siddiqi, for bringing her friendship into our studio as resident painter. Elizabeth and Geza von Habsburg, for their cozy guest room and late night talks. Vicky Colombet for her staggering work but also her quiet intellect; Kitty Hawks and Larry Lederman, who were there whenever I surfaced. Ben Taylor, and Marjorie Kaplan and Gus Szabo, all my surrogate siblings. My very first boss, Jane Isay, with whom I reconnected over this book.

My birthright sisters—my panel—Abby Ruddick and Lisa Ruddick, have always been there; their experience writing and publishing books before me helped me understand that it can be hugely rewarding; it can also be like filling out the world's longest form. The legacy we share from our parents is literally unfathomable—from our wild Canadian poet/woodsman/physician father, Bruce Ruddick, who once hung a deer leg outside our apartment window to age, but in many less odoriferous ways rooted us in the natural world even from the seventh floor; and our mother, Dorothy Ruddick, the obsessional Josef Albers–trained artist who worked most nights after I went to bed, so that the scratching sound of quill pen on watercolor paper—the sound of work—became a familiar, even comforting, backdrop to life. Our final time together spent on the Urban Garden Room—our first formal collaboration, at her life's end—was her last great gift to me. Both parents gave us a foundation in our life's work that allowed us to keep exploring, critiquing, teaching, and just never to imagine that we would ever, ever give up.

What we do is hard work. It requires knowing just enough about a huge number of topics. It requires a physicality—drawing, walking, breathing—that can keep us healthy. It requires that we be present, that we perform a kind witness. Raising children also draws on these skills, keeps us in the present, sometimes in awe. I feared when my daughter, Celia Placito, arrived that my work would never be the same. It never has been. It has been better—given the perspective and the love having children in our lives gives us. My son Jonathan Placito's attitude toward life—that he has won the lottery—is contagious, and has always buoyed me. I don't know what my work would be like without my two children. Less about life, most likely.

All of this work is the progeny of the true originals who hired me/us: Claire Weiss—a better design eye I have never collaborated with; Denzil deSouza, a true partner asking tough, tough questions; Cynthia and Ron Beck, exemplary stewards cultivating the next generation; Penny Lee, reclaimer of Queens Plaza; Fred and Nancy Poses, so far beyond being patrons of art that we need a new word; Frank Gallagher, Liberty State Park's steward/ecologist; for each one of the projects in this book there is a life, and a vision, that propelled us into a unique process, through a unique lens. This book is a testament to these optimists, and to the landscapes they love.

Illustration and Photo Credits

Any photos not listed are credited to the author

Preface

Page xi: J. Harrington - Massachusetts

Page xiii: Charlotte Barrows

Page xvi: David Kelly

Introduction

Page 2 left: *swethamushroom.wordpress.com*

Page 2 right: Marpillero Pollak Architects

Page 3 upper: Kim Soles

Page 3 lower: *Luxury Traveler*

Page 4: Jason Bregman

Page 7: Dave Bledsoe

Page 8: Margie Ruddick landscape

Page 10: commons.wikimedia.org

Page 11: *gossipsofrivertown.blogspot.com*

Page 13: Charles Birnbaum/The Cultural Landscape Foundation 2014

Chapter 1

Page 14: Steve Legato/New York Times

Page 17: Steve Legato/New York Times

Page 24: Steve Legato/New York Times

Page 40: Margie Ruddick landscape

Chapter 2

Page 44: Sam Oberter

Page 47: Marpillero Pollak Architects

Page 49 upper: New York Transit Museum

Page 49 lower: Penny Lee

Page 50: Courtesy of Van Alen Institute

Page 51: Penny Lee

Page 52 upper: Margie Ruddick landscape

Page 52 lower: Marpillero Pollak Architects

Page 53: Margie Ruddick landscape

Page 55: Marpillero Pollak Architects

Page 56: Marpillero Pollak Architects

Page 57: Marpillero Pollak Architects

Page 58 upper: Margie Ruddick landscape/Marpillero Pollak Architects

Page 58 lower left: Marpillero Pollak Architects

Page 58 lower right: Margie Ruddick/Marpillero Pollak Architects

Page 59: Marpillero Pollak Architects

Page 61: Penny Lee

Page 62 upper: Marpillero Pollak Architects

Page 62 lower: Tom Zook

Page 63 upper: Marpillero Pollak Architects

Page 63 lower left: Sam Oberter

Page 63 lower right: Steven Yavanian

Page 64 upper: Margie Ruddick landscape/WRT

Page 64 lower: Margie Ruddick landscape

Page 65: Margie Ruddick landscape/WRT

Page 69: Sam Oberter

Page 70: Marpillero Pollak Architects

Page 71: Marpillero Pollak Architects

Page 73: Margie Ruddick landscape/WRT

Page 74: Margie Ruddick landscape/WRT

Page 75 upper and lower: WRT/Margie Ruddick

Chapter 3

Page 76: Jason Bregman

Page 78: Betsy Damon

Page 85: Jason Bregman

Page 86: Betsy Damon

Page 87: Jason Bregman

Page 88: Jason Bregman

Page 89: Betsy Damon

Page 92: Margie Ruddick/Gensler

Page 93: Charlie fong 冯成 *via Wikimedia Commons*

Page 94: public domain

Page 96: SiChuan University

Page 97 upper: Betsy Damon

Page 97 middle and lower: Jason Bregman

Page 98: Jason Bregman

Page 99 upper and lower: Jason Bregman

Page 100: Jason Bregman

Page 101 upper and lower: Jason Bregman

Page 102: Jason Bregman

Page 104: Jason Bregman

Page 105 upper and lower: Jason Bregman

Page 106: Jason Bregman

Page 107: Jason Bregman

Page 108: Jason Bregman

Page 109: Jason Bregman

Page 110 upper and lower: Jason Bregman

Page 111: Jason Bregman

Page 112 upper: Jason Bregman

Page 112 lower: Jason Bregman

Page 114: Margie Ruddick/WRT

Page 115: Margie Ruddick/WRT

Page 117: Margie Ruddick/WRT

Page 118: Margie Ruddick/WRT

Page 119: Margie Ruddick/WRT

Page 120: Margie Ruddick/WRT

Page 121 upper and lower: Margie Ruddick/WRT

Page 122: public domain

Page 123: public domain

Page 124: Margie Ruddick/WRT

Page 125: Margie Ruddick/WRT

Page 126: Margie Ruddick/WRT

Page 127: Margie Ruddick/WRT

Chapter 4

Page 130: David Kelly

Page 132: public domain

Page 134: David Kelly

Page 135: David Kelly

Page 137 upper and lower: David Kelly

Page 139: David Kelly

Page 140: David Kelly

Page 143 lower: David Kelly

Page 144 upper left and right: David Kelly

Page 145 upper: Scott Frances

Page 145 middle: David Kelly

Page 145 lower left: David Kelly

Page 146 upper: David Kelly

Page 146 middle upper: David Kelly

Page 146 middle lower: Tom Zook

Page 148 lower: David Kelly

Page 150 upper and lower: David Kelly

Page 151 lower: Writer Corporation

Page 152 upper, middle, and lower left: Writer Corporation

Page 153 all photos: Writer Corporation

Page 154 lower: Writer Corporation

Page 156 lower: Writer Corporation

Chapter 5

Chapter 6

Page 194 right: Cloud 9/WRT

Page 195 upper: Cloud 9/WRT

Page 197 upper and lower: Cloud 9/WRT

Page 198 upper and lower: Cloud 9/WRT

Page 199 upper: Cloud 9/WRT

Page 199 lower: public domain

Page 200: John Hill

Page 201 upper: Karl Krause

Page 201 lower: public domain

Page 204: Dorothy Ruddick/WRT

Page 205 middle: Scott Frances

Page 206: Scott Frances

Page 207: Scott Frances

Page 209 upper: Scott Frances

Page 210 upper: Scott Frances

Page 217 lower: Scott Frances

Page 218 lower: Scott Frances

Page 222 upper and lower: Scott Frances

Page 223 upper: Scott Frances

Conclusion

Page 225: Jason Bregman

Page 226: Betsy Damon

Page 227: Jason Bregman

Page 228: Scott Frances

Page 229: Scott Frances

Page 230: Betsy Damon